FATS

Edible

Series Editor: Andrew F. Smith

EDIBLE is a revolutionary series of books dedicated to food and drink that explores the rich history of cuisine. Each book reveals the global history and culture of one type of food or beverage.

Already published

Apple Erika Janik *Banana* Lorna Piatti-Farnell
Barbecue Jonathan Deutsch and Megan J. Elias
Beef Lorna Piatti-Farnell *Beer* Gavin D. Smith
Brandy Becky Sue Epstein *Bread* William Rubel
Cake Nicola Humble *Caviar* Nichola Fletcher
Champagne Becky Sue Epstein *Cheese* Andrew Dalby
Chocolate Sarah Moss and Alexander Badenoch
Cocktails Joseph M. Carlin *Curry* Colleen Taylor Sen
Dates Nawal Nasrallah *Doughnut* Heather Delancey Hunwick
Dumplings Barbara Gallani *Eggs* Diane Toops
Fats Michelle Phillipov *Figs* David C. Sutton
Game Paula Young Lee *Gin* Lesley Jacobs Solmonson
Hamburger Andrew F. Smith *Herbs* Gary Allen
Hot Dog Bruce Kraig *Ice Cream* Laura B. Weiss
Lamb Brian Yarvin *Lemon* Toby Sonneman
Lobster Elisabeth Townsend *Melon* Sylvia Lovegren
Milk Hannah Velten *Mushroom* Cynthia D. Bertelsen
Nuts Ken Albala *Offal* Nina Edwards *Olive* Fabrizia Lanza
Onions and Garlic Martha Jay *Oranges* Clarissa Hyman
Pancake Ken Albala *Pie* Janet Clarkson
Pineapple Kaori O' Connor *Pizza* Carol Helstosky
Pork Katharine M. Rogers *Potato* Andrew F. Smith
Pudding Jeri Quinzio *Rice* Renee Marton *Rum* Richard Foss
Salmon Nicolaas Mink *Sandwich* Bee Wilson
Sauces Maryann Tebben *Sausage* Gary Allen *Soup* Janet Clarkson
Spices Fred Czarra *Sugar* Andrew F. Smith *Tea* Helen Saberi
Tequila Ian Williams *Truffle* Zachary Nowak
Vodka Patricia Herlihy *Water* Ian Miller
Whiskey Kevin R. Kosar *Wine* Marc Millon

Fats

A Global History

Michelle Phillipov

REAKTION BOOKS

Published by Reaktion Books Ltd
Unit 32, Waterside
44–48 Wharf Road
London N1 7UX, UK
www.reaktionbooks.co.uk

First published 2016

Printed and bound in China by 1010 Printing International Ltd

A catalogue record for this book is available
from the British Library

ISBN 978 1 78023 575 2

Contents

Introduction

Fats are essential for life. Along with protein and carbohydrates, they are the body's primary sources of energy. But
fats are not just about nutrition: they are also loaded with
cultural and symbolic significance. 'To chew the fat'; 'to butter
someone up'; 'fat cat'; 'fat chance'; 'to know which side one's
bread is buttered'; 'to grease one's palms'; 'to lard one's prose';
'to look as if butter wouldn't melt in one's mouth'; 'to pour
oil on troubled waters' . . . In popular phrases and idioms, fats
variously represent wealth, good favour, coldness, flattery and
bribery. Perhaps more so than any other food, fats are
ambiguous substances producing multiple meanings. These
meanings have been contested throughout history, in global
cuisines, in ongoing controversies about fats' effects on
health, in the practices of the food industry, and through the
representation of fats in contemporary art, literature and
popular culture. Fats have been understood as simultaneously
commonplace and decadent, linked to both power and
poverty, and associated with desire and with death.

While in common parlance 'fat' is often synonymous
with the fleshy corpulence of obesity, this book considers the
uses and meanings of culinary fats: that is, the kinds that are
ingested, rather than deposited on the body. As one of the three

vital macronutrients, fats exist in every corner of the globe where humans can be found. They appear in a myriad of forms and derive from a variety of origins, including land and sea animals, seeds, fruits and nuts. Fats are a class of chemical compounds called 'triglycerides', which are formed by the union of glycerol and three fatty acids. If solid at room temperature, these triglycerides tend to be referred to as 'fats'; if they are liquid at room temperature, they are normally called 'oils'. Typically, animal sources produce fats, while plant sources produce oils (with the exception of fish, which also produce oils).

Humans obtain fats and oils through a variety of mechanical and industrial means, including agitation (to make butter, for example), rendering (as in duck fat), pressing (such as for extra virgin olive oil) and extraction (for example, rapeseed/canola oil). But despite the differences in production methods and appearance, the culinary purposes and nutritional qualities of fats and oils are often similar. Both preserve and lubricate food, bringing richness and desirable textures to a range of dishes, as well as a sense of satiety. They also act as flavour carriers, coating the tongue and holding the flavour on your taste buds; they dissolve essential vitamins (A, D, E, K) and aroma compounds that are insoluble in water; and they provide essential fatty acids, which the body cannot synthesize on its own. As a vital source of nourishment, fats are both ubiquitous and universal, but their culinary pleasure also makes them luxuries. This is a book about the extraordinary life – simultaneously commonplace and remarkable, alternately banal and laden with meaning – of culinary fat.

I

Power and Prestige: Fats in History

Fats are more than simply foods to be eaten. Throughout human history, fat has been a symbol to be wielded. Fats have been integral to the reinforcement and regulation of cultural, social, religious and economic values, simultaneously symbolizing and bestowing power, authority, luxury and distinction.

Humans' larger brains and shorter digestive tracts mean that, biologically, we are much more dependent on nutrient- and energy-dense foods than other primates. At nine calories per gram, fat is much more energy dense than either protein or carbohydrate, which each consist of only four calories per gram. For most of the world's hunter-gatherer societies, fats play a crucial role. In most traditional diets, fats comprise between 36 per cent and 43 per cent of the diet by caloric intake,[1] but for some groups, the importance of fat is much greater. For example, the traditional Maasai diet is approx-imately 66 per cent fat calories, while the traditional diet of the Inuit is up to 70 per cent.[2] In cultures with a high reliance on animal-based food sources, the right balance of fat and protein is essential: a diet with insufficient fat can be fatal. During times of food scarcity – such as during the late winter and early spring of temperate and northern regions when

Inupiat seal hunter, *c.* early 20th century.

game animals are especially lean – excessive consumption of lean meat can result in a form of protein poisoning known as 'rabbit starvation', an agonizing and deadly condition in which sufferers experience intense pain and insatiable hunger. The Canadian explorer Vilhjalmur Stefansson, who spent many years with the native peoples of North America, observed their careful avoidance of overly lean meat, writing:

> Rabbit eaters, if they have no fat from another source – beaver, moose, fish – will develop diarrhoea in about a week, with headache, lassitude and vague discomfort. If there are enough rabbits, the people eat until their stomachs are distended; but no matter how much they eat they feel unsatisfied. Some think a man will die sooner if he eats continually of fat-free meat than if he eats nothing.[3]

Due to the essential nutrition fat provides, traditional societies have tended to favour the fattiest parts of the animal. The high value and desirability of fat, combined with its relative scarcity, means that within such societies fat operates as an important marker of social and cultural status. For many, it also functions as a vehicle through which power can either be conferred or diminished. A common practice in many parts of the world has been to give (male) hunters priority access to the fattiest, and hence most nutritionally valuable, portions of the animal, such as the bone marrow, the brain and the fat surrounding the kidneys and internal organs. Among the !Kung San of the Kalahari, where animal fat is scarce for much of the year, male hunters may be permitted to consume most or all of the limited yield of marrow fat and fatty organs while snacking at the kill site. Animal fat also goes primarily to the men of the Hadza in Tanzania, who similarly have preferential access to marrow fat at the kill. Among the Mbuti pygmies

Maasai warrior eating raw meat.

of the Congo, it is men who customarily receive the fat-rich brain of large prey animals.

Women's access to fat is often further inhibited by uniquely female food taboos. Among the Aranda people of Central Australia, for example, women are prohibited from consuming any meat or fat during the first months of pregnancy. In a number of Athapaskan societies of subarctic North America, pubescent girls are allowed to consume only lean, dried meat. Even among the Penan of Sarawak, on Borneo, where women have more equitable access to fat than in many other hunter-gatherer societies, fat is prohibited for lactating women. Indeed, some have argued that men's and women's differential access to fat has been instrumental in reinforcing patriarchal social structures in many traditional societies.[4]

In part due to this association with cultural value and (masculine) power, fat serves important ceremonial and ritual functions for a range of cultural groups. Traditional marriage ceremonies among the Maasai of Kenya and Tanzania involve the smearing of fat and oil from a male sheep on the bride's head and wedding dress. A widowed Maasai woman will customarily drink liquid fat as part of the rituals associated with the coming-of-age of her son: the fat acts as a laxative, with its expulsion from the mother's body symbolizing the expulsion of the impurities of the relationship with her son.

Fat has also traditionally been used to treat the much disputed 'Windigo psychosis' among the Algonquin people of North America. The Windigo, a malevolent cannibalistic spirit, was believed to possess human beings, giving them an intense desire for human flesh. Fat-rich foods, particularly bear fat and deer tallow, were given to those suspected of being afflicted. This was done not so much as a curative but as a test: fat was such an important and desirable commodity that anyone who rejected it had clearly ceased to be human and must be executed. As long as the fat was taken, there was still hope for recovery.

For the Kwakiutl (Kwakwaka'wakw) of British Columbia, fat was central to massive potlatches. These potlatches were social gatherings held to celebrate major life events, such as births, marriages and initiations, at which feasting lasted for days and enormous quantities of food were offered as a sign of the power and status of the host. When guests could no longer eat another morsel from among the mounds of seal blubber and eulachon (a type of fish) oil, the leftovers were burned in fires in a dramatic display of excess. Such feasts served as a form of one-upmanship among powerful Kwakiutl men, enabling them to improve their status rankings by placing guests in their debt.

The Kwakiutl were not the only ones to use potlatch-style feasting as a technique to shore up social status and power. For the ancient civilizations of the Fertile Crescent, palatial banqueting was used as a way to define and confer hierarchies. Meat, particularly fatty meat, was a key symbol of luxury and power at palatial meals. The royal banquets of Mesopotamia, for example, were gigantic fatty feasts. When the palace of the Assyrian king Ashurnasirpal II was completed in 879 BC, a ten-day feast for 69,574 guests included 1,000 fat oxen, 14,000 sheep, 1,000 lambs, hundreds of deer, 20,000 pigeons, 10,000 fish, 10,000 desert rats and 10,000 eggs.[5] In Bronze Age Greece, palatial feasting was an important tool for legitimizing elite authority. Banquet contributions of fattened livestock were obligatory for those of high status, while those of lower status made what contributions they could as a means of seeking favour. During the feasts, extravagant quantities of meat and fat were consumed. However, the bone marrow – an other- wise highly desirable source of animal fat – was burned as part of a ritual offering to the deities.

The ancient Sumerian Standard of Ur, displaying a banqueting scene, *c.* 2600 BC.

The royal banquet was a similarly important public relations exercise in imperial Rome, with opulent, fatty dishes – such as a whole pig stuffed with sausages and songbirds, and platters of birds' tongues – serving as symbols of the palace's wealth and authority. The excessiveness of such feasts was satirized in the *Satyricon*, attributed to Gaius Petronius and written during the age of Emperor Nero (first century BC). In one of the key scenes from the text, 'Dinner with Trimalchio', course after course is served with food that is not 'real' – that is, food masquerading as other animals or objects. From a whole pig, its insides bloated with fatty sausages and blood pudding designed to look like entrails, to pigeons moulded from lard (pork fat), the feast is a vulgar and nauseating display. Although written as a satire, the *Satyricon* was not an entirely wild exaggeration of feasting practices of the time. In a period when the ordinary population had limited access to meat and fat, extravagant feasting on such foods took on great symbolic power and significance.

Along with animal fats, olive oil was also an important tool in the demonstration of monarchical power. First cultivated by the inhabitants of Syria and Palestine at least as early as 4,000 BC, the olive created one of the foundational economies of the ancient world. Olive oil served as the backbone of the export trade, with the Greek trading posts of the Black Sea becoming an important hub for merchants from as far afield as the southern steppes of Russia. At Knossos in Crete, oil was the king's treasure and its export one of his major sources of revenue. Subjects of the Roman Empire were excused from military service if they planted a certain number of acres with olives. So important was olive oil to these ancient empires that the classical Greeks and Romans considered butter to be the food of barbarians – although in Mesopotamia, butter had been culturally significant enough to be depicted in Sumerian temple friezes from as early as 2500 BC.

In the medieval West, where feudalism, inclement weather and persistent warfare posed ongoing issues for food security, feasts were central to the social duties of the rich and powerful. Medieval lords used banquets to persuade the loyalties

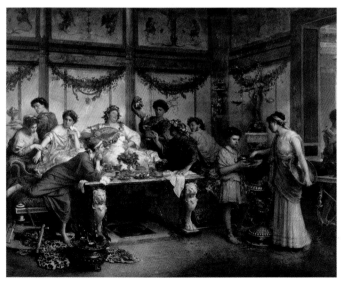

Roberto Bompiani, *A Roman Feast*, *c.* late 19th century.

and opinions of their guests. Domestic animals (cattle, pigs, sheep and goats), with their greater proportion of fat than game animals, were the most highly prized banquet foods. The lavishness of the table conveyed the wealth and power of the host. For example, during a feast at the French court in 1420, supplies of 100 fat oxen, 130 sheep, 120 pigs, 200 piglets, 60 fat pigs (for larding purposes), 200 kids and lambs, 100 calves, 2,000 poultry, 6,000 eggs and 1,600 kg (3,600 lb) of flour and cheese were used each day.[6] In cases when nobility entertained royalty, the expense and luxury of the feast items signified their loyalty and allegiance. The historian Pierre Jean-Baptiste Legrand d'Aussy (1737–1800) described a typical banquet hosted by the Count of Anjou in 1455 as including table decorations consisting of two enormous pies

> surmounted with smaller pies, which formed a crown. The crust of the large ones was silvered all round and gilt at

Large barrels known as *pithoi* were used in ancient Greece to store olive oil. These giant *pithoi* were found at Knossos palace, built in Crete *c.* 1900 BC.

the top; each contained a whole roe-deer, a gosling, three capons, six chickens, ten pigeons, one young rabbit, and, no doubt to serve as seasoning or stuffing, a minced loin of veal, two pounds of fat, and twenty-six hard boiled eggs, covered with saffron and flavoured with cloves.[7]

Fat was used as a tool of elite control not only in the extravagant display of the feast, but in the annual rents extracted from the peasants of the feudal estates. In cooler climate regions, these taxes were dominated by animal fats. The Frankish emperor Charlemagne (*r*. 800–814) stipulated the annual production and collection of sheep fat and beef tallow in the Capitulare de Villis, the court's manual for estate management and productivity. In Bavaria, butter and pork fat were included in peasants' annual burdens. The Saxon king Ina collected similar rents of butter and animal fat in the seventh century. With milking yields much lower than they are today, butter was an especially expensive fat to produce: between 9 and 35 litres (2–9 gallons) of milk were required to produce 1 kilogram of butter.[8] So while the food rents enabled the accumulation of food stores that likely protected feudal estates against the worst exigencies of famine, the annual burdens placed a heavy toll on the peasants, who suffered nutritionally from their limited access to dietary fat.

Historically, differences in social standing were expressed primarily through the access to, and display of, food in large quantity. By the seventeenth century, however, the manner in which food was prepared was becoming progressively more important. In western Europe, the previously dominant acidic sauces, based on vinegar or verjuice, were increasingly replaced with butter- and fat-based sauces that came to signify the luxury and opulence of aristocratic cooking. For example, seventeenth-century Florentine feasts continued to

Marie-Antoine Carême's designs for pastry decorations from *Le Patissier royal Parisien* (1854).

deploy vast amounts of food in the displays of wealth and power witnessed in previous eras, but the dishes served also highlighted the growing popularity of refined, butter-based cookery. The celebrations to mark the reluctant marriage of Marguerite-Louise d'Orléans to Cosimo III de' Medici in 1661 included an afternoon tea featuring no less than seven services, with the first service alone consisting of 35 separate dishes, many of them rich, fatty and buttery. Dishes included *capirottata* (roasted chickens and larded and roasted capons served with roasted sweetbreads); fat-rich mortadella sausage; salted and fried pigs' cheeks; and a shortcrust pie filled with candied citron, pistachios, marzipan, ham, roast capon breast, roasted sweetbreads, *agresta* (verjuice grapes), approval approval sugar and cinnamon. Plates of butter carved in the shape of a lion with a raised paw to represent the bride were also part of the banquet.[9]

Such ostentatious displays of wealth were typical of the ceremonial feasting of the Medici and the other grand families of the era, but throughout the seventeenth century and into the eighteenth, social distinction and power were conveyed increasingly through the cultivation of delicacy, rather than of excess. The French Revolution of 1789–99 accelerated the development of the restaurant trade in France and, with it, the emergence of *haute cuisine*. The closure of aristocratic kitchens had left the cooks of these grand households in search of work. Many of them became restaurateurs. This was the era of luminaries like Marie-Antoine Carême, who created beautiful and elaborate sculptures from lard, sugar and marzipan, and later, Auguste Escoffier, who elevated sauce making (and sauciers, or 'sauce cooks') to an area of specialized expertise. Escoffier, building on the earlier work of Carême, consolidated French cookery's varied and complex sauces to five key sauces: béchamel, espagnole, velouté, hollandaise and tomate. Each of these sauces included butter as a key ingredient, cementing the place of butter-based sauces as a characteristic of haute cuisine.

The expansion of the restaurant trade heralded the diffusion of elite food, with haute cuisine accessible not just to the aristocracy but to anyone who could afford it. Consequently, the restaurant became an important public site for the demarcation and affirmation of social status, particularly for the nineteenth-century bourgeoisie. Internationally, French cuisine became a model of culinary excellence, with 'classical' training for chefs still considered synonymous with 'French' cookery. Perhaps more so than any other ingredient, butter became a key symbol of classical French cuisine. The influence of Carême and Escoffier is still evident in the cuisine of contemporary chefs such as Joël Robuchon, awarded the Meilleur Ouvrier de France in cuisine in 1976 and recipient of Gault et Millau's 'Chef of the Century' in 1989, who popularized the mashed potato as a luxury dish: his extravagant *purée de pommes de terre* is famous for being loaded with butter.

Because of the historical associations with nutritional health, abundance and wealth, fats have operated as important symbols of utopia and paradise in a range of folklore and religious traditions. Stories abounded in medieval Europe of mythical places where food fell from the sky, pastries grew on trees and roast animals wandered about offering their meat to hungry inhabitants. These gastronomic paradises – known across artistic, literary and oral traditions as the land of Cockaigne – satisfied the dreams of a poor, deprived peasantry by offering images of abundance in which people never needed to go hungry again. In Scandinavian versions of the Cockaigne myth, rivers flow with sour cream. In French tales, houses are built of meat and trees are made from butter. German variations of the stories feature goats pulling cartloads of fat and salt, while hotcakes grow on trees.

More recent versions of the Cockaigne myth have also appeared in African American folk tales. In these tales, the mythical place of Diddy Wah Diddy is a gastronomic utopia for weary travellers: as they sit and rest, a baked chicken with a knife and fork stuck in its sides offers itself to be eaten, as does an endlessly replenished sweet potato pie. Depictions of Diddy Wah Diddy have appeared in a range of popular texts, such as in songs like 'Big Rock Candy Mountain', and in Disney's adaptation of the Br'er Rabbit tales, *Song of the South* (1946), which features a Garden of Eatin' containing baked hams, a chicken gravy river and a forbidden pork-chop tree. The different versions of the Cockaigne myth share in common an emphasis on meat and animal fats – foods that would have rarely featured in the diet of the poor and whose scarcity not

Pieter Bruegel the Elder, *Het Luilekkerland (The Land of Cockaigne)*, 1567.

only associated them with the wealthy and the powerful, but made them coveted objects of desire. The fatty indulgences offered by the lands of Cockaigne made them places of endless pleasure, satiety and celebration: not just temporary or fleeting feasts, but permanent places free of hardship.

Such desires for the pleasure and security of cornucopias of endless food are also reflected in conceptions of the afterlife in a range of religious traditions. From the Viking feasting halls of Valhalla to the Islamic paradise of Jannah, meat and fat are often the centrepieces of never-ending feasts. Fat is Jehovah's preferred food, with Leviticus 3:14–16 stipulating that the 'fat of the beast' be burned at the temple for His consumption. In Isaiah 34:6–7, acts of sacrifice are said to enrich the land through the introduction of fat, with the Lord rewarding His chosen people with rich, fertile soil. In fact, it has even been argued that the biblical reference to a 'land flowing with milk (*ḥālāb*) and honey' is more correctly translated in Hebrew as a 'land flowing with fat (*ḥēlebh*) and honey'.[10]

Due to the religious importance of fat, Jewish festivals are often observed by eating fat-rich foods. Since medieval times, the most desired celebratory dishes among Egyptian Jews use the rich tail fat of the fat-tailed sheep. In northern France, beef marrow is a delicacy. For the Ashkenazi Jews of Eastern Europe, schmaltz – rendered goose or chicken fat – holds a special place in feasting practices. Schmaltz was essential for the observance of kosher food practices in cold climates as it enabled adherence to prohibitions on the mixing of meat and dairy and on consuming foods from non-kosher animals in places where butter and lard were generally the fats of choice. Schmaltz is traditionally used in a range of festive breads and pastries. It is also used to fry latkes, the potato pancakes enjoyed during Hanukkah when fried foods are eaten to commemorate the miracle of the oil, in which a one-day supply of ritual oil miraculously burned for eight days. But fat's spiritual value also makes it the subject

German schmaltz on bread.

Carnival food in Santiago de Cuba, Cuba.

of religious food taboos. Kashrut (Jewish dietary law) prohibits the consumption of certain kinds of fat. *Chelev*, the suet that surrounds the kidneys, cannot be eaten; this fat is reserved for *korban*, a ritual burning or offering of food to the divine.

Christian traditions of Lenten fasting, during which luxury foods are given up as a form of penance, similarly highlight the careful regulation of fat consumption in religious communities. During Lent, a period of approximately six weeks leading up to Easter Sunday, foods including butter and animal fat are forbidden. 'Fat' or 'Shrove' Tuesday, the Tuesday before Lent, is a time to use up the fats in the larder. In the Protestant tradition, pancakes are a traditional way of emptying the larder of the fats prohibited during Lent. In the Catholic tradition, Fat Tuesday is celebrated with the festivals of Mardi Gras, the most famous of which is Rio de Janeiro's Carnival. It is a time for feasting on rich, fatty foods; in Brazil, these include *acarajé* (black-eyed bean fritters fried in *dendé*, or palm, oil) and *feijoada* (a hearty stew of black beans, beef, pork and lard).

Since at least the Middle Ages, it has been common practice for wealthy Christians to buy dispensations from the Church to avoid the religious obligations of Lenten fasting. One of the towers of France's Rouen Cathedral, reconstructed in 1506, is also referred to as the Tour de Beurre, or Butter Tower, because its building works were allegedly funded by donations from wealthy citizens made in return for permission to eat butter during Lent. For pious Christians who did not buy exemptions, fasting tended to conclude with large feasts. In France during the Renaissance, Martinmas (St Martin's Day) feasts included substantial quantities of goose fat. At that time, there was a belief that the further away from the earth a food was, the better its flavour would be, so birds – and geese in particular – were especially valued. Martinmas feasts also included the popular *menus oiseaux*, or 'bird menus': thrushes, blackbirds, nightingales, sparrows, buntings, finches, quail, ortolans, woodcocks and snipe confited in fat.

So central is fat to the symbolic repertoire of Christianity that Catholics even have patron saints of butter. Haseka, a thirteenth-century German ascetic who lived on whatever food was donated to her, was beatified by the Church when a gift of spoiled butter was made fresh in answer to Haseka's prayers. St Brigid of Ireland also experienced butter-related miracles: when an elderly woman appeared at her door begging for food, Brigid had little to give. But miraculously, her only remaining food – a dish of butter – multiplied to allow her share her meagre supplies with the woman in need.

The role of fats in religious iconography draws upon a broader history of the symbolic importance of fat, and of butter in particular. Butter represents fertility, prosperity and cleansing in a range of traditions. An Old English wedding custom saw newlyweds presented with a pot of butter to

Claude Monet, *Rouen Cathedral, West Façade, Sunlight*, 1892.

guarantee fertility. In Brittany, carved and decorated blocks of butter were displayed during wedding celebrations; these were later auctioned off with the proceeds going to the newlyweds. But people from parts of the world that prefer oil have traditionally viewed butter with great suspicion. Accounts of Provençal and Catalan travellers in medieval Europe suggest that many took with them their own olive oil for fear that the consumption of butter would make them vulnerable to leprosy.

As they do in Europe, fats occupy a prominent place in religious ceremonies in South Asia. In Indian Vedic ritual, ghee – a type of clarified butter, often spiced and/or cultured – is thrown into the fire as a source of sacred energy and as a re-enactment of Creation. This is because in Hindu belief, Prajápati, lord of creatures, sired his progeny by rubbing or 'churning' his hands together and pouring the resultant butter into fire. Ghee is thus a symbol of fertility and virility; at traditional Hindu weddings, male guests compete with each other to see who can consume the most ghee in one sitting as 'proof' of their virility. A fermented drink called *madhuparka*, made with ghee, honey, sugar and herbs, is traditionally offered to suitors about to ask for a girl's hand in marriage. Because it is made with the milk of the sacred cow, ghee has been used as a source of religious salvation to the higher castes. Food cooked in ghee becomes *pukka* – purified, acceptable to be eaten even by Brahmins, who otherwise adhere to a series of complex food rules and taboos. Ghee is also used to prepare breads and sweets to be served at temples and during festivals.

For the Sherpa people of Nepal, butter is used in a ritual offering to secure divine protection. The gods are presented with *tormas*, dough sculptures coated in coloured butter and ranging from several inches to several feet in height. An

Relief of Brahma as Prajápati, Government Museum, India.

Butter sculpture of the Tibetan sage Milarepa, thought to have lived from AD 1052 to 1135.

additional *torma*, called a *gyek*, is thrown out of the temple as food for the demons, in order to temporarily sate them and divert them from eating up the other offerings. In Tibet, butter is smeared on temple statues and used to create elaborate sculptures of the offering goddesses and other Buddhist symbols. Prior to the Chinese annexation of Tibet in 1951, dead lamas were embalmed in ghee according to traditional funeral rites.

Throughout history fats have been vital, and symbolically central, to many civilizations around the world, and there has consequently emerged a remarkably consistent set of religious and social systems associated with the regulation, circulation and consumption of these foods. This significance is also reflected in the different forms and methods of cooking, and cooking with, fats that exist across the globe.

2
Fats around the World: Cooking with Fat

Fats may have been deployed in the service of cultural, religious and economic practices throughout history, but their unique chemical properties have meant that they have also been put to a variety of other uses. Throughout the world, fats have been used to preserve and protect foods, create distinctive textures and flavours, and make the most of limited space, fuel and resources. Fats are not just symbolically significant, they are also highly versatile.

One of fat's oldest uses is as a preservative. From British potted meats and Flemish *potjevleesch* to French patés, terrines and rillettes, households have used fat's impenetrability to air as a means to preserve shredded and ground meats. The cooked meats are covered with a layer of warm liquid fat, which hardens as it cools, creating an airtight seal. Preserving with fat in this way has been used for centuries to extend the shelf life of perishable foods through the winter months. Today, many of these simple, ancient dishes are considered delicacies. *Confit de canard*, or duck confit, is now a staple on French restaurant menus throughout the world, but it originated as a method of tenderizing tough cuts of poultry and preserving them for long storage. To make a confit, legs of goose, duck or other wild game birds are gently simmered for hours in their own fat. The result is moist, tender meat and, when heated under a grill (broiled) or fried in a pan, deliciously crisp skin. Once cooled, the fat becomes solid, protecting the meat from airborne bacteria; individual pieces can be dug out as needed, leaving the rest intact. Meat confit is the centrepiece of a number of French regional specialities, perhaps the best known of which is *cassoulet*, a slow-cooked casserole from the rich agricultural region of Languedoc that also features a filling mix of haricot beans, sausage and fatty pork skin or belly.

Elsewhere in southern Europe and the Mediterranean, olive oil is the preferred fat for preserving seasonal vegetables, olives, cheeses, fish and herbs. The liquid oil performs a similar function to the solid fat atop preserved meats. Covering dried, pickled or brined ingredients with olive oil creates an airtight seal that prevents oxidation and retards mould growth. Many of the seasonal herb sauces found throughout the Mediterranean – pesto, *pistou*, *salsa verde* – are stored under oil to preserve the abundant but fleeting harvest of summer herbs. Indeed, many of the region's best-known appetizers –

Duck confit ready to be cooked.

Vegetables preserved in olive oil.

the oil-drenched olives, cheeses, tomatoes and peppers found in Spanish tapas, Italian antipasti and Greek and Middle Eastern meze – originally developed as a way of enjoying out-of-season ingredients throughout the year.

Prior to mechanical refrigeration, the consumption of highly perishable fats such as butter was primarily limited to cool climates. This is in part why liquid fruit and seed oils, such as olive, sesame, argan, groundnut and palm fruit oils, dominate the cuisines of the warmer regions of the Mediterranean, the Middle East, Africa and Southeast Asia. In cases where perishable fats are traditionally eaten in hot climates, fat functions not just as a preservative of other ingredients but as a food that must itself be preserved. This need to protect fat from spoilage has produced some unique products, including *smen*, a long-lasting, fermented butter used in Arabic and North African cooking. *Smen* is made by kneading clarified ewe's or goat's butter with salt and herbs before fermenting it in underground earthenware or stoneware pots. The *smen* is aged in these containers for months or even years. The result is a pungent concoction used to season couscous and tagines that, much like a rare aged cheese, is considered both a delicacy and a sign of wealth. In some parts of Morocco, aged *smen* is a feature of wedding day feasts and is traditionally supplied by the bride's family.

Another of fat's culinary uses is to protect delicate ingredients against the intense heat of cooking. Throughout Europe, very lean meats have traditionally been 'larded' by using a needle to weave long strips of fat through the meat. The fat melts into the meat as it cooks, adding moistness and flavour. A similar technique, known as 'barding', lays strips of fat over the surface of the meat. This fat is typically lard or bacon, but other fats, including caul fat, are also sometimes used. Caul fat is the fatty membrane that surrounds an animal's stomach; this lacy fat is used to wrap oven-baked meats and sausages, including traditional British faggots, French *crépinettes* and Italian *fegatelli*, melting completely into the dish as it cooks.

In other cases, it is fat's durability – its capacity to remain solid and waterproof, rather than to 'disappear' – that is its most desirable characteristic. The practice of buttering bread for sandwiches, for example, serves to provide a protective layer between the dry bread and the wet fillings. The prepar-ation of *smørrebrød*, the open sandwiches eaten in Denmark and throughout Scandinavia (*smörgås* in Sweden; *smørbrød* in Norway), always begins with a generous layer of butter spread over the bread base. This is then topped with a range of accompaniments: traditional *marinerede sild* (pickled herring) is popular, as is *dyrlægens natmad*, bread topped with liver paste, salt beef and onions; more contemporary versions include a variety of salads, eggs, cheeses and cold cuts. *Smørrebrød* were first popularized in the nineteenth century when factory workers were no longer able to go home for a hot midday meal, and so brought a packed lunch to work. Portable open sandwiches were ideal for this, as the thick layer of butter prevented the moist fillings from making the bread soggy before lunchtime.

Smørrebrød is just one of many examples of the importance of fats in the preparation of workers' meals designed to sustain long days of heavy physical labour. Because fats are both calorie dense and slowly digested, they are essential for long-lasting energy. It is for this reason that they are the centrepieces of many classic peasant foods. A traditional Norwegian breakfast consisting of a fat-rich combination of oily fish, cured meats, cheese, boiled eggs and bowls of sweetened sour cream was originally designed to sustain a long day's work on the land. Greek *lathera*, the widely eaten 'oiled' dishes in which vegetables are slowly cooked with tomato, herbs and a generous quantity of olive oil, first emerged as part of religious fasting practices, where the high fat content of the oil helped sustain farm workers and manual labourers during times when meat and animal fats were forbidden.

While some of the world's fattiest dishes, originally designed to provide essential sustenance for hunters, farmers and other labourers, are now considered out of step with con - temporary urban eating habits in many parts of the world, there are also many cases of these traditional dishes being 'rediscovered' and promoted as regional and national specialit - ies. Today, these dishes are not necessarily eaten to fuel heavy manual labour; they are enjoyed by expatriate communities nostalgic for a taste of 'home' as well as by gastronomic tour - ists seeking authentic regional flavours. For instance, the Bavarian *Jägerschnitzel* was once a typical meal eaten by hunters the night before an early morning chase (*Jäger* means 'hunter').

Danish *smørrebrød* topped with sprats, egg and cucumber.

This filling dish of crumbed and fried meat, creamy mushroom sauce and *Käsespätzle* (cheesy, hand-cut noodles) is now widely served to tourists and to locals in restaurants and brew houses across Germany, Austria and Switzerland.

Throughout Europe and the Middle East, hearty peasant meals once considered cheap and 'low class' offerings are now celebrated national dishes. In Hungary, fatty meat has traditionally been made into *pörkölt*, an inexpensive cattleman's stew spiced with onion and paprika. Along with goulash and chicken *paprikás*, *pörkölt* is now among Hungary's most famous stews. In Poland, *bigos*, a substantial hunter's stew, rich with several kinds of meat, sausage and sauerkraut, is today served as part of New Year's festivities. Lamb fat is the star ingredient of the Persian *dizi*, a high-calorie stew of beans, meat, potato and cubes of fat that was a traditional labourer's meal served in teahouses. Like many traditional foods, *dizi* is becoming popular again, particularly among the international Persian diaspora, who are the main customers for recent restaurant versions of the dish.

Other unique regional specialities that had fallen out of favour in recent years, such as the Italian *lardo* – so-called 'white prosciutto' – are similarly regaining prominence and popularity, in this instance through the work of the Slow Food movement. *Lardo*, made from pork back fat and cured in marble troughs with salt, herbs and spices, was traditionally eaten with bread, tomato and onion by quarry workers who needed a concentrated energy source to sustain intense fifteen-hour days cutting and hauling marble. Although it has been made since Roman times, changing work and dietary habits in contemporary Italy put *lardo* and *lardo*-making at risk of extinction. In 2004 it was listed as part of Slow Food's Ark of Taste catalogue of heritage foods and given IGP (Protected Geographical Indication) status, generating international interest in the product. Markets for *lardo* are now on the rise; it is even celebrated through its own annual festival that attracts international tourists each year to the Tuscan village of Colonnata.

Marble troughs used for curing *lardo di Colonnata*.

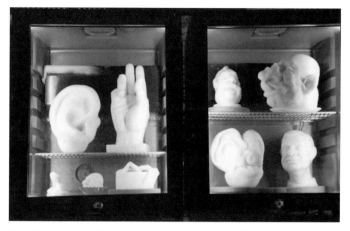

The Salo Museum-Café in Lviv is dedicated to the Ukranian delicacy *salo* in all its forms.

Salo, the Eastern European equivalent of *lardo*, has enjoyed a similar transformation from peasant food to celebrated national dish. In countries such as Ukraine, *salo* is traditionally made with pork fat preserved from feasts at Christmas and Easter – the only times of the year most peasant workers had access to meat. Calorie-rich *salo* was eaten with black bread, raw onion, garlic and pickles to fuel a day's toil in the fields. Today, however, its important place in Ukrainian food culture makes it a tourist attraction, with dedicated festivals in Lutsk and Poltava. It is also the subject of a museum-café in Lviv, which features a gallery of sculptures made from *salo* as well as a restaurant serving *salo*-based dishes, including a dessert made with *salo*, ice cream and fruit.

In addition to providing sustenance, fats are also enjoyed for the distinctive textures that they bring to dishes. The unique chemical properties of fats make them essential for baking, where they lend baked goods their appealing crispness and mouthfeel. Buttery biscuits, from Scottish shortbread

Butter lends biscuits such as shortbread their 'short', melt-in-the-mouth quality.

and German *Pfeffernüsse* to the Swedish *sandbakelser* and Norwegian *goro*, each get their dry, crumbly textures from butter's 'shortening' properties. That is, the fat, which is solid at room temperature, helps to 'shorten' the biscuit dough, inhibiting the development of the gluten in the flour. In contrast to bread doughs, in which the gluten is activated to produce a chewy, stretchy texture, dough enriched with fat produces a crisper, more tender final product. The shortening property of fat is an essential feature of flaky pastries, such as *wienerbrød*, a multilayered, sweet Danish pastry, and the French croissant, pain au chocolat and millefeuille. The distinctive texture of these delicacies is achieved by creating 'puff' pastry, which is made by layering the dough with butter (often a 50:50 ratio of dough to fat is used) and then rolling and folding several times. Classic puff pastry is made up of as many as 729 layers. The puffy, flaky quality of the pastry is the result of the water in the butter evaporating into steam during the baking process, causing the pastry sheets to crisp and separate into their individual layers.

If light and flaky French and Danish pastries are synonymous with butter, the hearty regional pastries of the British Isles are best known for their use of lard. Among the most well known of these is the Cornish pasty, which was popular among Cornwall's tin and copper miners, who needed a portable meal that they could carry with them to work; the pasty's thick, durable pastry was practical and convenient. Another well-known pastry is the pork pie, originally developed for the sustenance of the well-to-do English hunting set, who needed a snack that would be strong enough to survive a day's horse ride. Cornish pasties and pork pies are traditionally made with a lard-based, hot-water crust. Lard pastry tends to be sturdier than pastry made with butter, and retains its shape better. It also tends to brown less quickly, so it is ideal for pies that require longer baking and which need to survive rough transportation. In fact, lard pastry is so tough and durable that it is only relatively recently that the pastry casing has been

Making tarts with shortcrust pastry.

Butter is essential to the delectable, flaky texture of French croissants.

eaten at all – it once simply functioned as a portable container that was discarded once the filling within was eaten.

Many of the most desirable textures for baked goods are achieved when the fat is 'invisible' – that is, when its original form is unrecognizable in the finished product. For other types of cooking, however, fatty textures are often integral to the pleasure of the dish. Throughout Asia, for example, fats are valued for their textural qualities. In Japan, sushi made with the fatty belly of tuna, *otoro*, is a delicacy prized for its melt-in-the-mouth, creamy texture. In parts of China, fatty pork belly is braised to ensure that not all the fat is rendered out. Instead, the soft, sticky, gelatinous qualities of the fat and skin become integral parts of the meat's texture.

The smooth mouthfeel of many sauces and dressings is also the result of judicious use of fat. Plain cooked and raw vegetables are drizzled with oils – olive, sesame or chilli oils, depending on the cuisine – or oil-and-acid vinaigrette dressings to add flavour, lubrication and to mellow any overly bitter or pungent notes in the food. In classical French and European cooking, emulsified sauces and dressings are the most highly prized. Emulsification is achieved when fat molecules become evenly suspended within a liquid sauce. This is achieved through the use of heat, agitation and/or the addition of emulsifying ingredients such as flour, egg or mustard. The homogenization of the fat and liquid is what gives these sauces their luscious, creamy textures. One of the most widely used emulsified sauces is the thick white sauce béchamel, which begins with a roux, a cooked paste of butter and flour, to which hot milk is added. Béchamel is the basis of several traditional varieties of soufflé, as well as a key component of lasagne and moussaka. Another common sauce is hollandaise, made by gradually beating melted butter into egg yolks to form a creamy yellow sauce; mayonnaise is made in a similar way, replacing the melted butter with vegetable oil.

When preparing European-style emulsified sauces, a 'split' sauce is generally considered to be a failed sauce, but within regional cuisines elsewhere in the world, sauces in which the

Layering dough with butter to make puff pastry.

The hot-water lard pastry used to make pork pies is sturdy enough to survive a day's horse ride.

Sichuan *mala* hotpot with its characteristic layer of chilli oil and beef dripping.

oil has visibly separated from the other ingredients are often viewed as a sign of the dish's quality. In Sichuan cooking, for example, the *mala* ('numbing and spicy') hotpot features a thick layer of hot chilli oil and beef dripping (the fatty residue from roasted meats) slicked over its surface. Hotpots are dishes eaten communally in which raw meat, seafood and vegetables are cooked at the table in a pot of hot broth. They are eaten throughout China, but the hot-and-spicy *mala* hotpot is a speciality of Sichuan province. It was originally served as a cheap dish for dock workers, with the thick layer of oil helping to mask the unpleasant aromas of low-cost ingredients, which included solidified blood, beef tripe and kidney. Today, this layer of fat is considered one of the most pleasurable aspects of the dish, as it gives the otherwise plainly poached ingredients a smooth texture and a spicy, robust flavour.

Similarly, an authentic Thai curry or Malaysian laksa also has a layer of oil floating on its surface. This is achieved by

43

heating the coconut cream-enriched sauce until it 'cracks' – that is, until the coconut oil separates from the solids. This transparent layer of oil is able to take on more colour, flavour and aroma from the spices used than the previously homogeneous coconut cream. It is because of the need to crack coconut cream that curries and laksas can be difficult to replicate in a home kitchen. Since coconut cream can be cracked only under intense heat, these dishes are most ideally prepared in a wok over an open flame. The wok's ability to generate fierce heat allows it to produce flavours and textures that cannot be replicated through other forms of cooking; its curved base enables the flames to lick the sides of the pan, allowing the food to be heated quickly and evenly.

This also makes the wok ideal for cooking fast stir-fries and a range of other street food and hawker-style rice and noodle dishes. A traditional metal wok used on an open flame imparts unique flavour to dishes – what the Chinese call *wok hei*, or the 'breath of the wok'. This refers to the charred flavours that are characteristic of dishes ranging from the Cantonese stir-fry beef *chow fun* to the Malaysian noodle dish *char kway teow* and the Indonesian *nasi goreng* ('fried rice'). Each gets its distinctive smoky taste and lightly-charred-but-still-fresh texture from the wok's intense heat.

A cooking oil with a high smoke point is thus essential for wok-based cooking. Groundnut (peanut) and rapeseed oils are the preferred cooking oils throughout much of Asia as they are able to withstand the fierce temperatures of an open flame without burning or degrading. Many of these dishes begin with what the British food writer Fuchsia Dunlop – a specialist in Chinese cuisine – has described as 'frying-fragrant'.[1] This involves stir-frying aromatic ingredients, such as garlic, ginger and chilli, in the cooking oil until the oil has taken on their flavours. The other ingredients for the dish are then added to the wok and tossed in this flavoursome, fragrant oil. Dried chillies, fried-fragrant in this way, are what provide the distinctive scorched chilli flavour to dishes such as *gong bao* (kung pao) chicken, a stir fry of chicken, peanuts and Sichuan peppercorns. In Cantonese cuisine, cooks make optimum use of fried-fragrant oil by using an 'explosive' frying technique. When cooking shellfish, for example, the crustaceans are fried in the flavoured oil, heating them until the shells are almost red-hot. A sauce is then poured over the shellfish, which reacts explosively with the oil and allows the flavours to better penetrate the meat.

Frying is a highly effective method of heat transfer because fats and oils are able to reach more than double the temperature of boiling water, both cooking the food more quickly and contributing to the appetizing caramelization of its outer surfaces. This surface browning is the product of a chemical reaction known as the 'Maillard reaction', named after the French chemist Louis-Camille Maillard, who first described the phenomenon in 1912. The Maillard reaction occurs when the sugars and proteins in food break down through their contact with hot oil, creating a golden-brown colour and complex flavours that have been described by one professor of food science as 'some of the most delicious flavours known to man'.[2]

Some of the most delicious flavours and textures of all are produced through the Maillard reactions created by deep-frying food in fat. Completely immersing food in hot oil causes the moisture in the food to be rapidly converted to steam: this is the mass of bubbles you see when you first plunge food into the deep-fryer. This water vapour repels the oil from the food and prevents it from penetrating beyond the surface. The result is a crisp, brown crust and a moist, almost steamed, interior. Because it is a highly efficient and economical method of cooking, deep-frying has been a key cooking technique in the development of snack foods sold by street vendors and fast-food outlets throughout the world. Asian street food in particular highlights the many and varied delights of the deep-fryer, with snacks ranging from Indian samosas (fried, filled pastries) and puri (deep-fried bread puffs), to Filipino *kwek kwek* (quail eggs deep-fried in a bright orange batter), Japanese tempura (battered seafood or vegetables) and *takoyaki* (battered octopus balls) and Vietnamese *nem cua bê* (spring rolls).

Throughout Europe, the doughnut is among the most in-demand of the deep-fried snack foods. Popular versions include Dutch *oliebollen* (dumplings with dried fruit), Polish *pączki* (soft doughnuts filled with rose petal jam or plum preserve), Greek *loukoumades* (fried pastries soaked in honey syrup and sprinkled with crushed nuts and cinnamon) and churros (sausage-shaped doughnuts served with hot chocolate as a traditional breakfast food), which are popular in Spain and

Deep-fried delights, such as corn dogs, are a staple of American fairground food.

An open flame lends wok-fried food its characteristic smoky flavour.

Latin America. Other well-known snack foods in Latin America are empanadas (fried, filled pastries), tostadas (crisp fried tortillas) and *patacones* (deep-fried plantain). *Patacones*, like many of the traditional foods of Brazil, are deep-fried in *dendê* oil, a rich, vibrantly red oil derived from the fruit of the oil palm and also used in African cuisines, where deep-fried plantain is an equally popular snack.

But perhaps the foods most synonymous worldwide with the deep-fryer are American fast foods. Southern fried chicken, originating in the 'soul food' of African American slaves, is sold the world over through multinational fast-food chains. American fairgrounds are a cornucopia of deep-fried snacks ranging from corn dogs (battered and deep-fried hotdogs) to more unusual snacks such as deep-fried butter balls, deep-fried Oreos, deep-fried Twinkies and deep-fried Snickers bars. Demand for french fries has almost single-handedly changed the potato industry: the russet Burbank, with its ability to produce the long, golden, consistent potato strands so desired

47

by fast-food chains, is now the most widely grown potato variety in the world. America's reputation for 'supersized' high-fat fast-food is parodied by the Las Vegas burger chain Heart Attack Grill, which sells a range of Bypass Burgers (from the Single Bypass Burger to an Octuple Bypass Burger, depending on the number of beef patties and bacon slices), Flatliner 'world's highest butterfat content'. The restaurant was embroiled in international controversy following the heart attacks of an unofficial company spokesman and two of its customers.[3]

Deep-frying also features in American food trends such as the recent 'cronut' craze in New York; customers queue for hours outside Dominique Ansel's Manhattan bakery for a pastry that is a cross between a buttery croissant and a deep-fried doughnut. For the past several years, there has also been a trend towards deep-frying the traditional Thanksgiving turkey. A 10-pound (4.5-kg) turkey will cook in about 35 minutes when plunged into hot oil, compared to around three hours for oven roasting an equivalent-sized bird. Most cooks prepare this dish outdoors due to the large amounts of oil involved: deep-frying a 10-pound turkey requires up to 5 gallons (19 litres) of oil.

Given North America's reputation for high-fat fast foods and snack foods, it is perhaps fitting that health concerns about fats first originated there, leading to dramatic changes to dietary norms and food production practices in the West and elsewhere in the world since the 1950s.

3
Nutritional Science Weighs In: The Changing Fate of Fats

In the science-fiction comedy film *Sleeper* (1973), former health food shop owner Miles Monroe awakens from a 200-year coma in the year 2173 and requests a breakfast of wheat germ, organic honey and tiger's milk. His doctors are puzzled by his request, except for Dr Aragon, who remarks: 'Oh, yes! Those are the charmed substances that some years ago were thought to contain life-preserving properties.' 'You mean there was no deep fat?' asks an astonished Dr Melik, 'No steak or cream pies or hot fudge?' 'Those were thought to be unhealthy,' Aragon responds, 'precisely the opposite of what we now know to be true.' 'Incredible', Melik says.

In imagining a future in which hot fudge sundaes and deep-fried fat are revealed as the 'true' health foods, *Sleeper* offers an amusing, if barely concealed, barb at the apparent changeability of accepted medical wisdom: what might be deemed 'healthy' at one point in time is not necessarily considered so at another. That it is fatty foods that are the subject of *Sleeper*'s comedy is especially apt, given the changing attitudes to fat both before and after the film's release. Even today, ongoing concerns and disputes about the health effects of fats, particularly saturated fats, continue to perpetuate both lively academic debate and never-ending public confusion.

While fats have historically enjoyed prestige as high-value foods, their status – in the West, at least – plummeted dramatically after the Second World War. Since the turn of the twentieth century, improved life expectancy and the eradication of many serious infectious diseases led numerous medical experts to predict that America was approaching an unparalleled 'epidemic' of heart and other degenerative diseases. When Dwight D. Eisenhower suffered a severe heart attack in 1955 during his first term as u.s. president, it drew widespread awareness to the problem of heart disease. Following his recovery, Eisenhower replaced his previous penchant for high-fat foods – including his usual breakfast of bacon, sausages, porridge and hotcakes – with a low-fat diet and regular exercise, in line with the emerging medical consensus of the time.

The work of University of Minnesota researcher Ancel Keys was especially influential in establishing the connection between heart health and dietary fat. He observed that during the period of increased prosperity following the Second World War, Americans were eating more fat and red meat than was typical of their pre-war diets. Following his initial but brief Six Countries Study published in 1953, Keys commenced the now much-cited Seven Countries Study, a longitudinal study of the dietary habits of middle-aged men in the United States, Japan, Finland, the Netherlands, Greece, Italy and Yugoslavia. He found that populations with less heart disease, such as those in Japan, also tended to eat less saturated fat, whereas countries including the United States and Finland had both high levels of heart disease and diets high in saturated fat. As part of what became known as the 'diet–heart hypothesis', Keys concluded that saturated fats, such as those found in animal fats and tropical oils, raise blood cholesterol levels, increasing the likelihood of a coronary event; conversely, unsaturated fats, such as those found in nut, seed and fish oils, were thought to lower cholesterol levels and thus decrease the risk of heart disease.[1]

In 1961 Keys appeared on the cover of *Time* magazine in recognition of his pioneering research highlighting dietary saturated fat as the 'demon in heart disease'.[2] This, along with his best-selling book *Eat Well and Stay Well* (co-authored with his wife, Margaret, in 1959), led to the widespread popularization of Keys's work. Nonetheless, the 'diet–heart hypothesis' was not without criticism. Some argued that Keys's central studies failed to appreciate that fats are comprised of numerous fatty acids, and that the impact of these individual fatty acids on heart health cannot be identified when a person's diet is considered as a whole. Others highlighted methodological flaws, such as the study's reliance on what is known as an 'ecological fallacy', whereby incorrect conclusions may be drawn about individual people based on their group associations. The findings of the Seven Countries Study may show a correlation between dietary fat, cholesterol and heart disease, but they do not necessarily demonstrate a *causal* relationship. Such concerns were duly acknowledged and discussed, then quietly relegated to the background as 'anti-fat' health policy became official doctrine. Those who refused to accept the tenets of the diet–heart hypothesis found themselves quickly marginalized within the medical research community.

By 1977 recommendations to eat less fat had become formalized in the Dietary Goals for the United States (later to become the Dietary Guidelines for Americans), a set of principles created by a u.s. Senate committee and subse - quently adopted throughout the English-speaking West. These recommendations were summarized in the now-iconic food pyramid, which features breads and cereals at its base and advises that fats and oils be consumed only 'sparingly'. Between the 1950s and the early 1990s, the diet–heart hypothesis was endorsed and promoted not only by the major medical associations and governmental agencies, but by consumer advocacy groups, who targeted the food industry's use of saturated fats, including animal fats and tropical palm and coconut oils, in processed and fast foods.

In 1988 Philip Sokolof, a heart attack survivor and founder of the U.S. lobby group National Heart Savers Association (NHSA), called on the food industry to replace the saturated fats used in frying and food processing. His organization

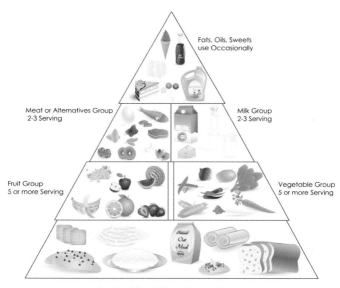

Fats, Oils, Sweets
use Occasionally

Meat or Alternatives Group
2-3 Serving

Milk Group
2-3 Serving

Fruit Group
5 or more Serving

Vegetable Group
5 or more Serving

Breads and Cereals Groups 5 or more Serving

Biology   Food Pyramid

The dietary guidelines outlined in the food pyramid have been adopted throughout the English-speaking West.

published full-page advertisements in the *New York Times*, *Washington Times*, *New York Post*, USA *Today* and *Wall Street Journal* featuring the slogan 'Who is poisoning America? Food processors are by using saturated fats!' The consumer advocacy group Center for Science in the Public Interest (CSPI) supported the NHSA's campaign through its own 'Saturated Fat Attack', which involved press conferences, letter-writing campaigns, petitions and advertisements. Nearly all the companies targeted by the NHSA and the CSPI, including Kellogg's, Carnation, Pepperidge Farm, Keebler, Procter & Gamble, Borden and Sunshine, responded by replacing animal fats and tropical oils with partially hydrogenated vegetable oils. Nabisco also voluntarily eliminated palm oil, coconut oil and lard from many of its products, including Oreos, Fig Newtons, Barnum's Animal Crackers, Ritz Crackers and Ginger Snaps, in response to the campaigns.

Pressure from the NHSA, the CSPI and a range of consumer groups contributed to major fast-food chains switching to partially hydrogenated vegetable oils for their deep-fat frying in the 1980s and 1990s. These partially hydrogenated oils allowed food processors to replace the texture, mouthfeel, shelf stability and cooking properties of animal fats and tropical oils but without the supposedly 'unhealthy' characteristics of saturated fats. Burger King made the switch to partially hydrogenated vegetable oils in 1986, as did McDonald's for everything except its french fries, which continued to be fried in beef tallow until 1991. Also in 1991 the American fast-food restaurants Dairy Queen, Jack in the Box and Wendy's similarly abandoned the use of animal fats and tropical oils in their cooking.

Although questions had been raised as early as 1959 about the potentially adverse health effects of the trans-unsaturated fatty acids associated with the manufacture of partially hydrogenated vegetable oils,[3] these oils were nonetheless widely considered to be a more benign alternative to saturated fats, a position that was repeatedly endorsed by the NHSA, the CSPI and much of the medical establishment at the time. In its 1986 *Fast Food Guide*, the CSPI described the shift from animal fats and tropical oils to partially hydrogenated vegetable oils as 'a great boon to Americans' arteries', and in its *Saturated Fat Attack* booklet of 1988 described partially hydrogenated vegetable oils as 'more healthful' than saturated fats. The effect of the CSPI's advocacy was striking: in 1982 a typical McDonald's meal of chicken nuggets, fries and apple pie contained 2.4 grams of trans fat, but after the change to partially hydrogenated vegetable oils, the same meal now had 19.2 grams of trans fat: a 700 per cent increase.[4] Indeed, during the 1970s and early 1980s, some margarines contained as much as 65 per cent trans fatty acids.

Two pivotal studies in 1990 and 1993, however, drastically changed the common view of partially hydrogenated vegetable oils as a 'great boon' for heart health. The first found that trans fatty acids may contribute significantly to the occurrence of cardiovascular disease by raising LDL (so-called 'bad') cholesterol and lowering HDL ('good') cholesterol levels.[5] The second showed that consumption of trans fatty acids in the form of partially hydrogenated vegetable oils was positively associated with cardiovascular disease.[6] Researchers have estimated that at least 30,000 heart disease deaths in the United States each year may be directly attributable to the trans fat content of processed and prepared foods, including margarines and other products containing partially hydrogenated vegetable oils.[7] Trans fats, it seems, were much worse than the saturated fats they were designed to replace.

As a result, one of the organizations that had been most influential in demanding the food industry's adoption of partially hydrogenated vegetable oils abruptly became one of its most scathing critics. The CSPI urged the U.S. Food and Drug Administration (FDA) to require labelling of trans fat content in foods. Following sustained campaigning, these recommendations were implemented in the United States in 2006 and have been followed by a number of other countries. Margarine sales went into freefall following the launch of the CSPI's anti-trans fat campaign in 1993, reaching a 70-year low by 2013.[8] In response to consumer concerns, Unilever reformulated its Promise margarines to be trans-fat-free in 1998, as did ConAgra Foods with its Fleischmann's margarines. In 2002 Frito-Lay eliminated trans fats from many of its snack products, including corn chips and cheese puffs.

In 2003 the organization BanTransFats.com brought a lawsuit against Kraft Foods requesting that the company cease and desist from marketing and selling Oreo cookies to children so long as the product contained trans fat. The case was dismissed after Kraft agreed to stop in-school marketing of Oreos and to introduce a line of the cookies that was trans-fat-free. In 2006 the CSPI filed a lawsuit against KFC for the use of partially hydrogenated oil in its deep-fried foods; this was withdrawn after KFC voluntarily elected to switch to trans-fat-free frying oil. Overall, the food industry's use of trans fats fell by at least half from 2001 to 2008.[9] Under continuing pressure from health and consumer groups, in 2013 the FDA issued a determination that trans fatty acids are not 'generally recognized as safe' (GRAS). The food industry is expected to phase out trans fat use within three years or to seek approval for their continued use under the classification of 'food additives'. Dairy products, of which trans fats are a minor (less than 5 per cent) but natural component, are unaffected.

At the beginning of the twenty-first century, the 50-year campaign against saturated fat appears to be in trouble. Such

WHAT ABOUT TRANS FATS ?

Cartoon by Ralph Hagen, 2006.

an abrupt about-turn in health advice has had a powerful impact on the public psyche. The discovery that the supposedly healthier partially hydrogenated vegetable oils were actually more dangerous than the saturated fats they supplanted has contributed to a growing distrust of established dietary advice. A major survey of UK residents in 2009 found that the majority of participants felt that scientists are 'always changing their minds' about healthy living advice. They perceived dietary advice to be constantly in flux, and so many believed that the best approach was to simply 'ignore it all and eat what you want'.[10] Today, butter consumption is at a 40-year high,[11] while palm oil – the 'unhealthy' saturated fat that trans fats once replaced in processed foods – is being used once more in a range of food preparations.

Nonetheless, proponents of the diet–heart hypothesis have been quick to remind the public of their achievements, particularly of the massive decrease in coronary deaths during the latter half of the twentieth century. However, the connection between this decrease in heart disease deaths and the adoption of 'low fat' dietary recommendations is not as clear-cut as it might at first seem. In fact, the claim that the post-war heart disease 'epidemic' was curbed through dietary change is a contentious one. In the United States, deaths from heart disease increased by 3.3 per cent between 1950 and

In 2006, the u.s. Food and Drug Administration required the trans fat content of all foods to be included on nutrition labels.

1967. After 1967, however, deaths started to sharply decrease, falling by 1.5 per cent each year between 1979 and 1997.[12] This has often been attributed to the dietary changes that also occurred during this time: between 1979 and 1997, Americans' intake of saturated fats was in decline. But a closer look at the data reveals that while deaths may have decreased, the overall *incidence* of heart disease did not. The decline in heart disease deaths is likely the result of more effective clinical interventions, improved surgical techniques and advances in intensive care, rather than of dietary changes. In fact, recent data suggests that cardiovascular disease remains on the rise in the West, even as death rates continue to decline.[13]

At best, this rising incidence simply reflects the limited role of dietary changes in stemming the tide of cardiovascular disease; at worst, it is one of the unintended consequences of this change. Many experts now believe rising rates of heart

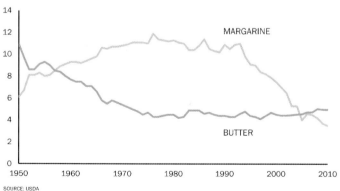

Butter and Margarine Consumption
US per-capita consumption of butter and margarine in pounds per year, 1950-2010

SOURCE: USDA

U.S. per capita consumption of butter and margarine per year, 1950–2010.

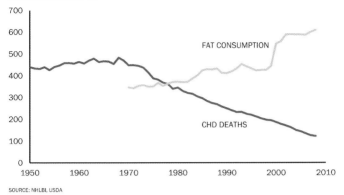

Fat Consumption and Coronary Heart Disease Mortality

US age-adjusted coronary heart disease deaths per 100,000 population vs total fat calories consumed per person per day

FAT CONSUMPTION

CHD DEATHS

SOURCE: NHLBI, USDA

U.S. age-adjusted coronary heart disease deaths per 100,000 population versus total fat calories consumed per person per day.

disease to be one of the devastating unanticipated effects of the diet–heart hypothesis. A 2013 review blames the substitution of partially hydrogenated vegetable oils for animal fats and tropical oils, observing that:

> The introduction of PHVO [partially hydrogenated vegetable oils] into the human food chain, and the associated increase in intake of TFA [trans fatty acids], may well have contributed significantly to the high levels of CVD [cardio - vascular disease] mortality and morbidity in much of the 'Western' world in the post-war era.[14]

In 2005 the chair of the Department of Nutrition at the Harvard School of Public Health, Walter Willett, told the *New York Times* that he now regretted the advice that he had given patients to replace saturated fats with partially hydrogenated vegetable oils:

When I was a physician in the 1980s, that's what I was telling people to do [replace saturated fats with partially hydrogenated vegetable oils] and unfortunately we were often sending them to their graves prematurely . . . In reality, there was never any evidence that . . . trans fat[s] were better than butter, and as it turned out, they were actually far worse.[15]

But there were also other adverse health consequences associated with the widespread recommendations to reduce saturated fat. To the food industry, the diet–heart hypothesis offered a remarkable opportunity to market a series of 'low-fat', 'fat-reduced' and 'heart-friendly' product lines. Because they need to replicate the desirable flavours and textures of their full-fat counterparts, many of these products use large amounts of sugar and other carbohydrates to compensate for the lack of fat. 'Low-fat' or 'fat-reduced' products are not necessarily 'low calorie', with a number of reduced-fat product lines containing the same or even more calories than their original full-fat equivalents. This is especially a risk for some types of reduced-fat or non-fat yoghurt, which, though low in fat, can often be high in sugar. Since the 1950s, average daily calorie intake in the United States has risen significantly, with a threefold increase in sugar consumption in the last 50 years.[16] While fat's energy density has long been perceived as fattening, many experts are now pointing to the role of excess carbohydrate consumption in escalating global obesity rates. According to the World Health Organization, obesity is now at epidemic proportions, with over 300 million obese adults worldwide.[17] Overconsumption of refined sugars and processed carbohydrates are now thought to lead to a range of significant health problems, including weight gain, insulin resistance and raised levels of saturated fatty acids in the bloodstream.

While the diet–heart hypothesis has raised the public profile of heart disease, it may also have contributed to a paradoxical situation in which obesity rates are on the rise even as fat consumption is on the decline. With rising obesity rates perhaps one of the unintended consequences of recommendations to reduce dietary fat, the much-maligned low-carbohydrate diet movement has been notably successful in challenging the conventional wisdom by using fat as a weight loss tool. In 1953 A. W. Pennington published a study in the *Journal of Clinical Nutrition* that proposed that weight loss was best achieved not by a low-fat, calorie-controlled diet, as was the dominant view at the time, but by a calorically unrestricted diet high in both fat and protein but very low in carbohydrates.[18]

Fran, 'Strict Diet', 2004.

By 1963 these findings had come to the attention of clinician Robert C. Atkins, who was struggling with his own weight issues at the time. Atkins had such remarkable success on Pennington's weight loss plan that he started to actively promote the diet to his patients and to the public through appearances on the *Tonight Show* and in *Vogue* magazine. Atkins enjoyed such popularity that when he published *Dr Atkins' Diet Revolution* in 1972, the book became an instant best-seller. Atkins's diet diverged from most mainstream diet plans in that it urged dieters to be 'unafraid of natural fat', including in the forms of butter, cream, cheese, olive oil and fats from meat, poultry and fish, describing this eating plan as an 'alliance with Mother Nature'.[19] Natural fats were promoted as beneficial for weight loss and for overall health because they were sustaining, protected against rapid spikes in hunger and blood sugar levels, and enabled dieters to avoid the dangers of 'fake foods' laden with 'chemically altered trans fats'.[20] His remarkable success saw the updated *Dr Atkins' New Diet Revolution*, published in 1992, sell over 15 million copies. It also paved the way for the popularity of a range of other low-carbohydrate diets in the late 1990s, including the South Beach, Zone and Protein Power diets. Remarkably, Atkins had achieved a level of popular credibility despite strident criticisms from the medical community. In 2002 he featured in an issue of *Time* under the heading 'People Who Mattered'.

Current dietary guidelines in the English-speaking West still recommend reducing dietary fat, but they also now advise replacing both saturated and trans fats with polyunsaturated and monounsaturated fats and oils. The recently revised Australian Dietary Guidelines suggest replacing high-fat foods that contain predominantly saturated fats, such as butter, cream, cooking margarine, coconut oil and palm oil, with foods that contain predominantly polyunsaturated and monounsaturated fats, such as oils, spreads, nut butters/pastes and avocado.

The National Heart Foundation of Australia similarly describes saturated and trans fats as 'unhealthy' fats that should be avoided, and encourages the consumption of 'healthier fats includ[ing] monounsaturated fats and polyunsaturated fats'. Such distinctions between 'good' and 'bad' fats are thought to explain the comparatively lower rates of coronary heart disease among traditional Mediterranean populations (hence the recent promotion of the so-called 'Mediterranean diet') as well as among those, such as Japanese and Arctic populations, that traditionally consume large quantities of fish: the protective effects of the 'good' fats found in olive oil and marine fats are thought to be beneficial to heart health.

However, some have pointed to the limitations of talking about fats as 'good' or 'bad', or characterizing certain foods as containing 'saturated', 'polyunsaturated' and 'monounsaturated' fats. This is an overly simplistic way of thinking about foods and their effects on health. After all, rather than comprising only one type of fat, foods always contain several types. Saturated fat's rigid molecular structure would make a purely saturated fat completely inedible, so foods necessarily contain saturated and unsaturated fats in combination. For instance, the fats found in lard are approximately 39 per cent saturated, 45 per cent monounsaturated and 11 per cent polyunsaturated.[21] As one Scottish research team remarked, what does it mean to say that 39 per cent of the fat is damaging to the cardiovascular system, while the other 61 per cent is protective?[22] Do the different types of fats cancel each other out?

Consequently, despite apparent consensus within mainstream dietary advice, the diet–heart hypothesis remains

Dietary guidelines recommend consumption of 'healthy' mono- and polyunsaturated fats, such as those found in nuts and avocados.

contentious. As early as 2001, a meta-analysis of 27 studies examining the relationship between dietary fat and heart disease concluded that

> Despite decades of effort and many thousands of people randomized, there is still only limited and inconclusive evidence of the effects of modification of total, saturated, monounsaturated, or polyunsaturated fats on cardio-vascular morbidity and mortality.[23]

A decade later in 2012, the same research team updated its research with new findings, but once again failed to find any significant effect of dietary fat intake on cardiovascular mortality.[24] Another meta-analysis published in 2010 and incorporating 21 studies and 347,747 research subjects also found no significant evidence that saturated fat is associated with an increased risk of heart disease.[25]

In 2014, in a project led by the University of Cambridge and partly funded by the British Heart Foundation, Rajiv Chowdhury and colleagues published the most extensive and comprehensive review of the relationship between dietary fat and heart health to date.[26] Their huge database comprised 45 observational studies and 27 randomized trials on coronary heart disease risk based on diet data from more than 600,000 people in Europe, North America and Asia. They found that dietary intake of trans fatty acids was associated with a 16 per cent increase in heart disease risk, and that two omega-3s – the polyunsaturated marine oils docosahexaenoic acid, or DHA, and eicosapentaenoic acid, or EPA – were associated with a lower risk of heart disease. Otherwise, the study found no evidence that saturated fat increases the risk of heart disease or that so-called 'good' polyunsaturated and monounsaturated fats have any protective effects on the heart.

The olive oil consumed as part of the traditional Mediterranean diet is thought to have beneficial effects on heart health.

There were strident criticisms of each of these studies. The reaction to Chowdhury's work was especially swift. Walter Willett stated publicly that the research should be retracted. 'They have done a huge amount of damage', he told *Science* magazine. 'I think a retraction with similar press promotion [to the original article] should be considered.' The association Dietitians of Canada also issued a statement rejecting the study: 'Unfortunately, this review gives newspapers more fodder for turning nutrition guidelines into further skepticism for consumers'. Defending his study, Chowdhury argued:

> In 2008, more than 17 million people died from a cardiovascular cause globally. With so many affected by this illness, it is critical to have appropriate prevention guidelines which are informed by the best available scientific evidence.[27]

Similar sentiments were expressed by Ron Krauss, director of atherosclerosis research at the Children's Hospital Oakland Research Institute, in relation to his 2010 publication in which he claimed that the large volume of studies linking saturated fat to heart disease risk was primarily the result of publication bias rather than unequivocal scientific evidence: in other words, he argued, research that supports the dominant view is more likely to be accepted, while findings that challenge that view are less likely to be published.[28]

So while in 1973 *Sleeper*'s depiction of cream pies and deep-fried fat as 'health foods' offered an amusing jibe about the changeability of nutrition advice, it seems that today we are still unsure about what is or is not healthy. While it was perhaps not the 'great boon to Americans' arteries' it was once thought to be, the fear of fat has certainly been a great boon to the food industry, which developed an array of new products and manufacturing processes that have profoundly changed everyday eating habits throughout the West.

4
Manufacturing Fats: Low-fat, No-fat, Artificial Fat

Health concerns about dietary fat have revolutionized the contemporary food industry. Throughout the West, super-market shelves are bursting with a multitude of products claiming to offer health benefits to consumers: 'low fat', 'no fat', 'no cholesterol'. Practices of agriculture and meat production have also seen profound changes, with the development of new oil seeds and animal breeds that comply with changing cultural expectations about dietary fat. While health concerns have led to dramatic changes in the nature of contemporary food systems, food production practices and everyday eating habits over the past few decades, many of these 'alternative' products have much longer histories. In fact, for more than a century food manufacturers have been replacing animal fats with a range of other substances for reasons of cost, shelf stability and convenience. It is only recently that concerns about dietary fat have offered the food industry the marketing triumph it hoped for, turning these products from inferior substitutes to highly desirable and profitable commodities.

Food industry practices of substituting animal fats for alternatives first became widespread in the nineteenth century, when industrialization and urbanization posed nutritional problems for Europe's growing numbers of city dwellers. Dietary fat in the form of meat and dairy products was becoming increasingly expensive and inaccessible to lower-income households. By the second half of the nineteenth century, exploding populations had resulted in a crisis of supplies of edible fat. France was especially desperate. Bismarck's militarization of Prussia and the impending Franco-Prussian war was putting pressure on France's military forces. In 1866 Napoleon III launched a competition as part of the Paris International Exposition to discover a 'product suitable to replace butter for the navy and the less prosperous classes of society'. It was stipulated that the product be 'inexpensive to manufacture and capable of being kept without turning rancid in flavour or smelling strong'.[1]

Hippolyte Mège-Mouriès responded successfully to the challenge in 1869. The French chemist had developed a butter substitute made from caul fat of beef, combined with cow's udder and skimmed milk, which he named 'oleomargarine' after mistakenly believing the mixture contained margaric acid. By 1871 Mège-Mouriès had sold his patent to the Dutch company Jurgens (later to become part of the conglomerate Unilever). Oleomargarine had better keeping qualities than butter and could be sold at about half the price, but it initially made only a modest impression on the market. It was not until 1910, following the introduction of hydrogenation techniques, that margarine gained wider popularity as a butter substitute.

The development of margarine heralded the emergence of industrial food production in which only large, heavily capitalized enterprises could participate in its manufacture. Margarine's industrial origins meant that the product was met with suspicion and alarm, particularly by the dairy industry, which saw margarine as a threat to the livelihoods of dairy

Making
oleomargarine,
1880.

farmers. Uniting as part of a powerful lobby, the dairy industry claimed that margarine caused indigestion and other
ailments, and that it contained diseased and putrid beef, dead
horses, dead hogs, dead dogs, mad dogs and drowned sheep.[2]
The unsavoury reputation of the meatpacking industry,
one of the worst in the nineteenth century, did not help the
public image of margarine.

In 1902 – in an address to the u.s. Senate – Wisconsin
senator Joseph Quarles described margarine as repulsive and
unnatural, contrasting it with wholesome and bucolic images
of butter produced by dairy cows chewing the cud in green
pastures:

> Things have come to a strange pass when the steer com-
> petes with the cow as the butter maker. When the hog
> conspires with the steer to monopolize the dairy business,
> it is time for self-respecting men to take up the cudgels

for the cow and defend her time-honored prerogatives
. . . We ought not now to desert her or permit her to be
displaced, her sweet and wholesome product supplanted by an artificial compound of grease that may be
chemically pure but has never known the fragrance of
clover, the freshness of the dew or the exquisite flavor
which nature bestows exclusively on butter fat to adapt
it to the taste of man . . . I desire butter that comes from
the dairy, not the slaughterhouse.[3]

Intense lobbying from the dairy industries in the United
States, Canada, New Zealand and Australia was successful in
limiting the market for margarine. The dairy industry's
political influence was one of the earliest examples of
powerful groups and organizations successfully lobbying to
shape the legislative agenda. Until the 1950s, margarine was
subject to discriminatory taxation in the United States in
order to mitigate the product's market advantage in terms of
price. Bans on yellow colouring were also in place to ensure
that margarine could not be sold as, or be mistaken for,
butter. Margarine's unappetizing natural colour posed a
problem for the margarine industry; some American manu -
facturers responded by including capsules of yellow colouring
that customers could knead in to the margarine at home. In
some states, bans on yellow colour remained in place until
the late 1960s. Five states, including Vermont, New
Hampshire and West Virginia, passed legislation requiring
that margarine be dyed pink. In Canada, the sale of margarine
was under total prohibition until 1949 (with a brief exception
between 1919 and 1922), and bans on yellow colouring were
repealed in Ontario only as recently as 1995 and in Quebec as
recently as 2008. In New Zealand, margarine was available
only on medical prescription, and could not be coloured

Vintage cigarette packet immortalizing Hippolyte Mège-Mouriès, the inventor of margarine.

Dutch margarine advertisement, *c.* 1893.

fried foods healthful as well as delicious

Fried foods can be as healthful as they are delicious, if you fry them in Crisco, the strictly vegetable cooking fat.

Crisco makes fried foods wholesome because it is wholesome itself. It is simply a solid white cream of nutritious vegetable oil—delicate, appetizing, pure, white, tasteless, odorless. It does not turn rancid.

Everyone can enjoy Crisco-fried foods. They are as easily digested as if they were baked.

Get Crisco from your grocer—one pound, net weight, or larger sizes. Always packed in this sanitary container—*never sold in bulk.*

Do you know how to make your family's meals healthful, as well as appetizing?

"Balanced Daily Diet" tells you about the food elements that build the healthiest bodies, and gives a simple rule for planning meals so they contain these elements in the proper proportions, yet include only foods you like. It also gives many delicious recipes and daily menus. Written by Janet McKenzie Hill, founder of the Boston Cooking School, and editor of "American Cookery." To get this valuable book, send only 10 cents postage, with your name and complete address, to Department F-3, The Procter & Gamble Company, Cincinnati, Ohio.

Use Crisco for all kinds of cooking. It makes tender, flaky, digestible pastries and biscuits. It enriches the most delicate cakes so that they taste as good as if they were made with butter. Yet Crisco is as economical a cooking fat as you can use.

Vintage Crisco advertisement, *c.* 1920s.

yellow, until 1971. In Australia, prohibitions on yellow colouring were lifted in the 1960s, but it was not until the late 1970s that margarine replaced butter as the most widely consumed spread.

In the United States, margarine's fortunes had improved two decades earlier. Butter shortages during the Second World War enabled margarine to gain a foothold in the American market, with margarine sales overtaking those of butter by the 1950s. By this time, the composition of margarine had changed dramatically since its original invention, having been transformed from a product made from animal fat to one based on vegetable oils.

The first product to be widely adopted for household and commercial uses was Crisco shortening. Developed as a lard substitute by Procter & Gamble in 1911, Crisco was originally made from partially hydrogenated cottonseed oil. Procter & Gamble launched a series of high-profile advertising campaigns emphasizing Crisco's pure, all-vegetable composition, in an attempt to distinguish it from the less illustrious origins of margarines made with animal products. Procter & Gamble also distributed a free cookbook containing 615 Crisco recipes. Crisco was a great success, with initial sales of 1,200 tonnes in 1912 skyrocketing to 27,000 tonnes by 1916.[4] When in 1914 another shortening, Kream Krisp, also made of partially hydrogenated cottonseed oil, emerged on the market as a serious competitor to Crisco, Procter & Gamble filed for patent infringement. They had lost the claim by 1920 but the Brown Company, which manufactured Kream Krisp, was financially ruined and eventually sold out to Procter & Gamble. But while Crisco was able to neutralize the commercial threat posed by Kream Krisp, in losing the case they also lost their claim to a monopoly on the hydrogenation process.

THAT'S RIGHT, spread it on thick as you like!
Good, good margarine. Tastes so fresh,
so wholesome! And it *is* wholesome, too!
Packed through and through with nutrition.
Plenty of Vitamin A the year around. And don't
forget nutritious margarine saves money—
a lot of money for the usual-sized family.
Spreads easily, even at normal refrigerator
temperatures. Millions of people are finding
there's no substitute for margarine—
the smoothest spread to put on bread!

*The staff of life
needed around the world—
don't waste a precious crumb.*

This Seal means that all nutritional state-
ments made in this advertisement are acceptable to the Council on Foods and Nutrition of the American Medical Association.

Nutritious **Margarine**

NATIONAL ASSOCIATION OF MARGARINE MANUFACTURERS
Munsey Building, Washington 4, D.C.

American margarine advertisement, *c.* 1940s.

Eventually, this opened the way for soybean producers to
dominate the market for partially hydrogenated vegetable oils
and shortenings, following the collapse of the cotton industry
in 1968. By the 1950s, consumption of soybean oil in the U.S.
rivalled that of cottonseed oil, but until the late 1940s the price
of soybean oil had been continually discounted in order for

it to compete with cottonseed and corn oils, at a cost to growers of up to \$90 million annually.[5] Because of its high content of polyunsaturated linoleic and alpha-linolenic fatty acids, soybean oil has a tendency to develop 'grassy' or 'paint-like' smells on standing – odours that consumers tended to find much more objectionable than those produced by rancid cottonseed or stale corn oils. Hydrogenation significantly curtails these odours by reducing the undesirable components of oils, alpha-linolenic acid in particular.

Hydrogenation is a chemical process whereby hydrogen gas, in the presence of a metal catalyst, is used to increase the saturation of unsaturated fatty acid molecules. By altering the levels of saturation, vegetable oils – especially soybean and canola oils – become less prone to oxidation and rancidity and are able to be heated to higher temperatures without degradation. The market dominance of vegetable oil-based margarines and shortenings was thus due not only to their uptake by households seeking inexpensive butter substitutes, but to their use by the food manufacturing industry.

The cost, transportability and stability of these industrially manufactured fats make them highly desirable to the food industry. Since most fried snack foods contain 20 to 40 per cent oil, fats play an essential role in determining the storage stability of industrially fried food products.[6] These products must sustain weeks and even months of warehousing, distribution, storage and sale without losing freshness. Oil used in industrial frying must have good stability in order to ensure the required shelf life for products. These characteristics can be achieved through the partial hydrogenation of vegetable oils.

Of course, any benefits of vegetable shortenings to the food industry were moot once they were revealed to be likely sources of trans fats. Sales of margarines and shortenings plummeted while commercial applications also decreased as fast-food outlets and food processors shifted to no- or low-trans fat oils. 'Trans fat-free' alternatives, mostly based on palm oil and high-oleic rapeseed (canola) oil were widely adopted, with the market share of soybean oil dropping from 76 per cent to 64 per cent between 2005 and 2010.[7] New types of genetically modified soybeans, such as soybeans with more than 75 per cent oleic acid (a similar composition to olive oil), are currently being trialled. The American Soybean Association strongly resisted bans on trans fats, arguing that they would lead to increased consumption of saturated fats, greater reliance on imported palm and rapeseed (canola) oils, and would jeopardise innovative techniques such as interesterification. Eliminating the use of partially hydrogenated vegetable oils in processed foods is predicted to result in a financial loss to domestic soybean farmers of $1.6 billion.[8] In 2014 there were approximately 1 million tonnes (2.5 billion pounds) of partially hydrogenated oils still being used in the u.s. in households and by the food industry.[9]

As well as motivating a shift away from partially hydrogenated vegetable oils, health concerns have also assisted in growing product lines of so-called 'functional foods'. Functional foods are foods with ingredients added to provide a specific health benefit. For instance, products such as eggs, beverages, margarines and infant formulas are fortified with fish oils and omega-3 fatty acids with the aim of improving the health (and, often, the 'intelligence') of consumers. Cholesterol-lowering margarines, which claim to reduce cholesterol by up to 10 per cent, enjoy a notable share of the spreads market. One of the first products to be released on that market, Benecol, was a hit in its native Finland when it was introduced in 1995, selling 165 million servings in its first few years – no

Vintage Kream Krisp advertisement, *c.* 1919.

mean feat for a country with a population of only 5 million people and a product that was six times more expensive than regular brands.[10] The active ingredients in cholesterol-lowering margarines are plant sterols and stanols, which are isolated from vegetable oils (soybean, rapeseed/canola, corn) or from 'tall oil' (a by-product of the manufacture of wood pulp); the sterols and stanols are thought to inhibit the absorption of cholesterol in the intestine. Fortified margarines, health drinks and yoghurts can cost up to four times the price of their non-sterol/stanol competitors; however, recent European research conceded there was little evidence to indicate clinical benefit from their use.[11]

But of all the nutritional modifications, it is fat reduction that has proved to be the most common and the most profitable. Because fat is vital to the flavour and texture of foods, the development of new manufacturing techniques were needed to produce low-fat foods that still mimicked the sensory qualities of fat. The most popular reduced-fat products – skimmed, low-fat and no-fat milks – require the least processing, but even these include additional milk proteins and milk solids to replace the body and mouthfeel of higher-fat milks. Reduced-fat foods frequently contain a greater proportion of air and/or water than their full-fat counterparts, requiring manufacturing processes that, for example, create products with smaller bubbles or droplet

Industrial frying oils must be able to withstand high heat without degrading.

Supermarket display of margarines and butter spreads, Australia.

sizes in order to offer the illusion of richness and creaminess, as is the case for reduced-fat ice creams, mayonnaise and desserts.[12] Other snack foods, processed dairy products and dressings include gums, emulsifiers and bulking agents, including xanthan gum, cellulose, polydextrose, carrageenan, starches and dextrins, to give foods the structure, opacity, tenderness, viscosity and creaminess of fat.

In 1988 the United States had around 2,500 fat-reduced products for sale. By 1992 food processors were introducing new fat-reduced products at a rate of almost 2,000 annually.[13] However, following the introduction of over 5,400 new products lines between 1995 and 1997, they quickly realized that they had pushed the low-fat concept too far. Consumers, finding the taste of the new fat-free and low-fat foods unpalatable, were increasingly reverting to higher-fat or full-fat product lines; so significant was this trend that average daily fat consumption increased by 16 per cent between 1997 and 2000.[14] To maintain sales many companies reformulated their products to contain more fat. For example, Nabisco reformulated its SnackWell's line of low-fat and fat-free products, announcing that 'our consumers are willing to accept up to an additional gram and a half of fat because they want great taste first.'[15]

As well as reduced-fat products, fat replacers, including fat substitutes and fat mimetics, were an innovative way in which the food industry responded to calls for 'healthier' processed foods in the late twentieth century. Unlike fat-reduced products, fat substitutes alter the caloric value of fat without compromising flavour or texture. However, the success of these products has been limited, due to intensified consumer opposition to 'industrial' solutions to health problems following the trans fat fiasco. Consequently, only one fat substitute, Benefat (the brand name for 'salatrim', short- and long-chain acyl triglyceride molecules), which claims 6 calories per gram instead of the usual 9 calories, is currently being marketed as a reduced-energy fat – although recent research has called into question Benefat's original reduced-energy claims.[16] Benefat is used in a variety of baked goods, dairy products and confectionary lines, but is un-suitable for frying.

Perhaps the best-known fat mimetic is olestra, marketed by Procter & Gamble as Olean. Discovered accidentally by Procter & Gamble researchers in 1968 while trying to find a fat that could be easily digested by premature infants, olestra is a sucrose polyester – a sugar-based compound that mimics the sensory and physical properties of fat, but contains no caloric value. This is because olestra cannot be absorbed from the stomach and therefore passes through the body undigested. A 30-gram (1-ounce) bag of potato chips normally contains about 10 grams of fat and a total of 150 calories, while the equivalent olestra product contains around 9 grams of fat but only about 70 calories.[17] Olestra's additional advantage is that it has the cooking properties of natural fat and oil, and so can be substituted for any conventional oil in the production of fast foods, fried foods, restaurant meals and industrially manufactured foods.

Despite Olean's apparent benefits, Procter & Gamble faced an especially long battle to bring it to market, in part because there were significant regulatory challenges for this type of product. As a result of this unique situation, the FDA was required to establish new regulatory standards for products that could not be tested in routine ways. In 1996, nearly 30 years after Procter & Gamble initially sought approval, olestra was approved for use in savoury snacks only – although the FDA also required products to be fortified with additional vitamins and to be labelled with a warning about the possible side-effects of olestra consumption: 'This Product Contains Olestra. Olestra may cause abdominal cramping and loose stools. Olestra inhibits the absorption of some vitamins and other nutrients. Vitamins A, D, E, and K have been added.'

In 2003 Procter & Gamble successfully petitioned the FDA to have the warning label removed on the grounds that these gastrointestinal complaints were not supported by available evidence and that the public could misconstrue the warning to believe that no vitamins would be absorbed when consuming olestra. Procter & Gamble also felt that the label had a negative impact on product sales. Nevertheless the FDA's decision to allow the removal of the warning labels was probably too late for Procter & Gamble, which had spent some $500 million just bringing the product to market.[18] Although sales were predicted to reach $1 billion by the end of 1999, Olean fared much worse than expected, with sales levelling off at about $50 million annually.[19] Just like Benefat, olestra had limited appeal for today's consumers. Continual criticism by groups such as the CSPI did not help.

Modified-fat products, functional foods, fat substitutes and fat mimetics are designed to offer 'healthier', lower-fat food options, but these modified foods are often heavily processed, top-of-the-food-pyramid snacks – what the journalist Michael Pollan would describe as not 'food' but 'edible foodlike substances'.[20] Pollan is one of the best-known advocates for the 'real food' movement, a diverse collection of groups and individuals committed to the preservation of traditional food cultures and artisanal food practices and opposed to the nutritional, culinary, cultural and environmental impoverishment of contemporary industrial food systems. Proponents of the real food movement reject the notion that existing industrial food systems can provide the solutions for healthy and nutritious eating, and instead propose alternative food systems based around the values of quality, sustainability and community.

'Real food' is that which is closest to its original form; an 'edible foodlike substance' is that which has been 'processed to the extent that it is more the product of industry than of nature'.[21] For the real food movement, 'empty calories' in these edible foodlike substances have added to the overexpansion and negative environmental impacts of industrial farming and agriculture, as well as to the expansion of Western waistlines (with its attendant chronic diseases, including heart disease and diabetes). The fact that industrial food products such as partially hydrogenated vegetable oils had previously been marketed by the food industry as 'healthy' when they are anything but has contributed to growing consumer scepticism and distrust of the ethics and safety of the food industry and existing industrial food systems. This has in turn boosted markets for minimally processed foods. Butter and lard are

Monsanto's 'Roundup Ready' oilseed rape (canola) has been highly controversial.

now back in fashion, with u.s. sales at a 40-year high.[22] Markets for cold-pressed olive, peanut, sesame, safflower and sunflower oils are also growing.[23] Cold-pressing produces oil by mechanical means rather than by methods of chemical extraction, and so does not use the solvents or intense heat needed to remove oil from seeds like rapeseed (canola) or soybeans.

Cold-pressed oils have also been adopted as an alternative to genetically modified (GM) oil seeds. By some estimates, up to 60 per cent of processed foods in the United States contain some genetically modified ingredients, much of it coming from the oils used in food manufacture.[24] 'Roundup Ready' versions of rapeseed, soybeans, corn and cotton have been manufactured by the Monsanto Company since the 1990s. These crops are augmented with a gene that enables them to tolerate the herbicide Roundup, a product also marketed by Monsanto. Worries about the safety of GM oils, objections to the corporate control of food systems and concerns about the environmental consequences of contamination of

Factory equipment for olive oil production.

non-GM crops by wind- or insect-pollinated GM crops have mobilized diverse groups in opposition to genetically modified foods. In many parts of the world, it is a statutory requirement to label food products that contain genetically modified organisms, but for the five largest producers of GM crops – the United States, Argentina, Brazil, Canada and China – no such regulations exist. In parts of the European Union and Australia, concerns about GM foods have resulted in bans and moratoria preventing the introduction of genetically modified crops and promoting alternative methods of food production, including of edible oils.

Concerns about the sustainability of industrial food systems have also contributed to emerging markets for free-range and heritage-breed meats. For decades, lean animals have dominated the commercial market, largely on the grounds that customers were seeking to eat less saturated fat. It was only by breeding leaner pigs, for example, that pork could be plausibly marketed as 'the other white meat' (that is, equivalent to lean chicken breast). In recent years, however, heritage-breed pigs have been making a comeback. Breeds such as the Berkshire and the Wessex Saddleback, raised by small farmers in free-range conditions, are slower-growing than the breeds used in conventional pork production and have a characteristic thick coating of fat that gives the meat greater flavour and moistness. Both pig varieties are classed as critically endangered. Many breeders argue that the very survival of these breeds depends on increasing demand for their meat. The dilemma was characterized by Eliza Wood, an Australian breeder of Wessex Saddlebacks: 'we have to eat their bacon to save their bacon.'[25]

The altered composition of fats and oils in processed foods, the increased use of vegetable oils (and decreased use of animal fats) and changes in animal breeding practices are each startling examples of how health fads can profoundly modify the food chain. The food industry's 'solutions' to health problems have had significant impacts on what we eat and

Wessex Saddleback pigs.

how that food is produced – not to mention the paradoxical effects on the health conditions that the 'solutions' attempted to combat. The lasting consequences of this are inscribed not just on our own bodies but in the practices of the food systems and industries that feed us.

5
Desire and Defilement:
Fats in Popular Culture

In part because of their longstanding connections with health, death, power and decadence, fats are important sources of symbolic value in popular culture. From wartime children's stories featuring extravagant fatty feasts, to literary depictions of fats as motifs of sexual and racial oppression, to the impact of more recent television cooking shows and celebrity chefs on popular attitudes towards cooking with – and eating – fat, fats lead symbolic 'double lives' both as sources of desire and comfort and as objects of excess and defilement.

Fats offer fantasies of plenitude in children's tales, in part because fats provide warmth, nourishment and experiences of eating that were outside the everyday dietary realities of many readers. Hot buttered toast simulates the cosy comforts of home in Kenneth Grahame's pastoral tale *The Wind in the Willows* (1908). When Toad's misadventures find him miserable and lonely in prison, the jailer's daughter revives his spirits by bringing him toast dripping with butter. The toast is so laden with butter that it runs through the holes of the bread in 'great golden drops, like honey from the honeycomb'. Its impact on Toad is dramatic:

> The smell of that buttered toast simply talked to Toad, and
> with no uncertain voice; talked of warm kitchens, of

breakfasts on bright frosty mornings, of cosy parlour firesides on winter evenings, when one's ramble was over and slippered feet were propped on the fender; of the purring of contented cats, and the twitter of sleepy canaries.[1]

The Wind in the Willows' depiction of a mythical golden age of English rural life in which communities existed in tune with the natural world gained popularity among urban audiences in the throes of the overpopulation and widespread malnutrition that gripped England's cities at the turn of the twentieth century.

Food has often been referred to as the 'sex of children's literature',[2] in part due to the lengthy descriptive passages objectifying food and eating, turning them into objects of fetish. Enid Blyton's stories are littered with memorable scenes of lunches, afternoon teas and midnight feasts in which children with huge appetites gorge themselves on large quantities of sweet and fat-laden foods. Blyton's books were most popular during and after the Second World War, when the average weekly ration consisted of meat up to the value of 1 shilling and sixpence, 8 oz (220 g) of sugar, 4 oz (110 g) butter or fat, one egg and 1 oz (30 g) of cheese. This is much less than is needed for even a day's worth of meals in many of Blyton's stories, particularly her series set in the Malory Towers and St Clare's boarding schools, which are littered with descriptions of plentiful meals. Typical of these is the delightful afternoon tea served by Clarissa's old nanny in *Upper Fourth at Malory Towers* (1949), which features a spread of

> tongue sandwiches with lettuce, hard-boiled eggs to eat with bread-and-butter, great chunks of new-made cream cheese, potted meat, ripe tomatoes grown in Mrs Lucy's brother's greenhouse, gingerbread cake fresh from the

oven, shortbread, a great fruitcake with almonds crowding the top, biscuits of all kinds and six jam sandwiches![3]

In Blyton's tales, feasting is not simply a fantasy of plenitude but an indicator of good character. Generosity with food is often a sign of virtue; in contrast, stinginess – with butter in particular – is a clear sign of villainy. In one of the Famous Five books, *Five Run Away Together* (1944), Mrs Stick serves the children sandwiches that are 'too stale; there was not enough butter inside, and they were far too thick'.[4] Unsurprisingly, she is later revealed to be a crook.

While in some stories fats signify utopian abundance in times of austerity, in other stories fatty foods symbolize deception, danger and evil. Cautionary tales of unfettered decadence abound. In Disney's 1940 retelling of Carlo Collodi's *The Adventures of Pinocchio* (1883), disobedient boys are lured to Pleasure Island, where they are given the freedom to destroy furniture, smoke cigars and stuff themselves with all foods imaginable. Their gluttony is represented primarily by fat-laden foods, with Pinocchio eating a large ice-cream cone from one hand and a whole pie from the other. But the apparent pleasure of their limitless freedom is false: the boys' gluttonous behaviour ultimately transforms them into donkeys to be sold as slaves to salt mines and circuses. In the Brothers Grimm's 'Hansel and Gretel' (1812), children are similarly lured into danger by greed: this time, by the witch's tempting gingerbread house. But while Hansel and Gretel are punished for their unchecked appetites through their capture and imprisonment, it is the witch's calculated gluttony that is the sign of her irredeemable evil. Not content to merely eat the children once she has captured them, the witch delays eating Hansel for four weeks, holding him captive and forcing Gretel to cook for him in order to fatten him up. This desire for fattened meat – to eat for pleasure, rather than to satisfy hunger – is what signals the witch's irreparable wickedness, which can be expunged only by her death in the flames of the oven at the conclusion of the story.

In children's stories, fatty foods are frequently used as vehicles through which we are made to consider the pleasures and dangers of indulging one's appetites; in some stories, though, fats are also a means to symbolically represent and explore racial and economic oppression. In *The Story of Little Black Sambo* (1899) by Helen Bannerman, the theft of the South Indian boy's new clothes by tigers prompts a series of events that results in the animals melting away into a pool of butter. Sambo's family collects this butter to make pancakes – a feast that satiates the whole family, but particularly the young boy, whose intense hunger requires 169 pancakes to be satisfied. While the book has been controversial owing to its racist terminology and its representation of the black child as 'greedy', Sambo's greed can also be interpreted as a reasonable response to racialized inequalities of food access and distribution.

Economies of food also dominate African American folk tales, such as the Br'er Rabbit tales, which often include the stealing of food. In contrast to Little Black Sambo, who was victorious over the tigers that stole from him, Br'er Rabbit is a trickster who consistently outwits those he steals from. In African and African American oral traditions, the trickster is often a morally ambiguous character – simultaneously villain and folk hero – whose actions are determined by an ethic of self-preservation that compels him to go to extreme lengths to protect himself from various forms of subjugation and disempowerment. The Br'er Rabbit tales, circulated in African American oral slave traditions, present Br'er Rabbit's trickster behaviour as a legitimate response to various forms of

Gluttony is punished in the Brothers Grimm's story of Hansel and Gretel.

inequality, including unequal food distribution. The stories were collected by Joel Chandler Harris and published in *Uncle Remus, his Songs and his Sayings* (1881); in them, Br'er Rabbit regularly steals food from the plantation owner Farmer John and his sometime adversary Br'er Fox, and Br'er Rabbit's kind-hearted and trusting friend Br'er Possum frequently pays the price. In one of the tales, 'Mr Rabbit Nibbles up the Butter', Br'er Rabbit sneaks away from Br'er Fox and Br'er Possum to secretly eat additional portions of Br'er Fox's butter. Having eaten all the butter, Br'er Rabbit smears the residue onto the mouth of a sleeping Br'er Possum, blaming him for the illicit butter consumption. Backed into a corner, Br'er Possum suggests a 'test' to determine the true culprit: they should build a fire and attempt to jump over it. The thief, heavy with butter, would presumably fall in the fire and be revealed as guilty. Br'er Rabbit and Br'er Fox jump over the fire with ease, but the luckless Br'er Possum falls in and burns to death.

In another tale, published as 'Workin' with Butter', Br'er Rabbit and Br'er Possum have a job stacking butter into crates for Farmer John. Br'er Rabbit, unable to stop himself despite Farmer John's threats of death, consumes large quantities of the butter. When he returns, a furious Farmer John demands that both Br'er Rabbit and Br'er Possum kneel down and turn their backsides to the sun, so that the butter would leak out, thereby revealing their guilt. Again, Br'er Rabbit smears the melted butter on Br'er Possum to avoid blame, but unexpectedly begs Farmer John not to kill Br'er Possum, tricking him into throwing them both into the briar patch, from which they both easily escape. In contrast to European folk tales, whose moral messages tend to be more absolute and in which Br'er

E. W. Kemble, 'Br'er Rabbit and the Tar Baby', 1904, illustration.

Rabbit's behaviour would more likely have been constructed as a punishable offence, there is a greater moral ambiguity in the Br'er Rabbit tales. His tendency to steal food from others is figured not as a condemnable greed but as a struggle to obtain a greater share of the available resources, and as a reasonable form of resistance to unjust systems of racial, economic and gastronomic oppression.[5]

Butter also functions as a vehicle for the symbolic playing out of racial tensions in adult literature and film. The film *Butter* (2011) satirizes the racism and conservatism of the American Midwest in its depiction of a showdown between competitive butter carvers at the Iowa State Fair. Butter sculpture – a phenomenon popular at American state fairs since the 1900s and a characteristically 'white' social activity – represents social climbing, local celebrity and a potential route to public office for Laura Pickler (Jennifer Garner), the trophy wife of Iowa's long-reigning champion butter carver, Bob. With her disdain for the 'liberal media', her aspirations to reach the White House and her refusal to apologize for being 'white and tall and pretty', Laura's character parodies Tea Party types such as Sarah Palin and Michele Bachmann. However, Laura's ambitions are thwarted by the arrival of a ten-year-old African American orphan, Destiny, whose natural flair for butter art and bewilderment at the cut-throat politics of the butter scene ('white people are weirdos', she concludes) lampoons small-minded Republican values.

In Toni Morrison's *Beloved* (1987), butter literalizes the oppression and sexual violence of slavery in more dis-turbing ways. When Paul D sees Halle for the last time at the ironically named Sweet Home plantation, he is sitting at the butter churn, smearing the butter on his face. The butter is a substance associated with the sexual violence experienced

Butter sculpture by Jim Victori and Marie Pelton, Harrisburg, Pennsylvania, 2013.

by his wife: Halle had witnessed the schoolteacher's nephews brutally taking his wife Sethe's milk, and his inability to protect his family drives him to madness. Sethe learns years later that Halle had witnessed her violation, and that this was why he had failed to meet up with her during their escape from Sweet Home. Now, whenever she recalls Halle, she has the image in her head of him at the butter churn:

There is . . . my husband squatting by the churn smearing the butter as well as its clabber all over his face because the milk they took is on his mind. And as far as he is concerned, the world may as well know it.[6]

In *Beloved*, butter expresses Halle's anguish at the dehumanization of slavery, but in other texts butter becomes a tool, rather than simply a symbol, of sexual and racial violence. For example, butter is the lubricant for the anal rape scene in the film *Last Tango in Paris* (1972), in which the American Paul forcibly sodomizes the Frenchwoman Jeanne, making her repeat after him: 'The children are tortured until they tell their first lie . . . the will is broken by repression . . . freedom is assassinated.' Jeanne's treatment at the hands of Paul is one of the film's many tacit references to the French military's torture of Algerians, conflating sexual and racist violence.

Such images of depravity, however, are tempered by the more celebratory ways in which butter is depicted in other popular texts. In *Julie and Julia* (2009), butter is the ultimate expression of gustatory pleasure. The film introduces us to Julia Child (Meryl Streep) (1912–2004), the doyenne of American television cookery, through her first encounter with the dish sole meunière: inhaling its delicious scent deeply, she murmurs, ecstatically, 'Butter.' It also dramatizes New York author Julie Powell's (Amy Adams) attempt to cook all the recipes in Child's *Mastering the Art of French Cooking*, and sees her stock her fridge full of butter, marvelling at the delights of cooking with such huge quantities of fat. As she says:

Let me say this: is there anything better than butter? Think it over: every time you taste something that's delicious beyond imagining and you say, 'What is in this?', the answer is always going to be 'Butter.' The day there's a

meteorite heading to the earth and we have 30 days to live,
I am going to spend it eating butter. Here's my final word
on the subject: you can never have too much butter.

Fittingly, Julie's final 'gift' to Julia at the conclusion of the film
is to leave a block of butter in front of Child's portrait at the
Smithsonian National Museum of American History, which
houses her kitchen.

But no fictional character or food personality loves fat
more than Homer Simpson. Homer's eating habits are relent-
lessly mocked in *The Simpsons* (1989–), in which his enjoyment
of outlandishly fatty foods satirizes an American culture of
excess and overconsumption. In one episode, Homer skips
church to make his 'patented space-age out-of-this-world
moon waffles' – a caramel waffle wrapped around a whole
stick of butter. 'Mmm, fattening', he says as he downs the

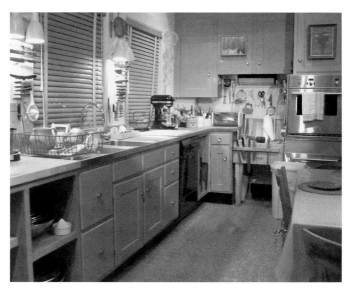

Julia Child's kitchen, Smithsonian National Museum of American History.

Homer Simpson's appetite for outrageously fatty foods satirizes the excesses of American culture.

sickening concoction. In another episode, Homer salivates over an advertisement for the Good Morning Burger, which consists of 18 oz (500 g) of minced beef, soaked in butter and topped with bacon, ham and a fried egg.

In 'King-Size Homer', he embarks on a plan to gain 61 lb (28 kg) in order to qualify for disability provisions that would enable him to work from home. He visits Dr Nick

Riviera – a graduate of Hollywood Upstairs Medical College – who introduces him to the 'food-rubbing test': 'Remember,' Dr Nick tells him, 'if you're not sure about something, rub it against a piece of paper. If the paper turns clear, it's your window to weight gain.' At Krusty Burger, Homer and Bart test this method using a fish sandwich: rubbing the burger against the wall turns the bricks into a transparent window. Like a gas-guzzling SUV, Homer's insatiable and indiscriminate appetite represents the greedy overconsumption of white Middle America. It also reflects an abject corporeality – a rendering of Homer's grotesque excesses in the very form and shape of his body. In 'King-Size Homer', his massive weight gain leaves him largely confined to his house, dressed in an absurd floral muumuu and with fingers too fat to use the phone (he does, however, ultimately save the town by using his enormous girth to plug a leak in Springfield's nuclear reactor).

Janine Antoni, *Gnaw*, 1992.

Nina Sellars with *Blender*, 2005.

The abject qualities of fat are also explored in contemporary art, where it has been used to represent transformation, flux and the socially produced sanctions placed on the body. In feminist performance art, for example, fat is often used to explore female desire and critique the cultural construction of feminine beauty. The 1990s saw the emergence of a number of artists who used their bodies to expose or highlight the contemporary conditions of women. Janine Antoni's *Gnaw* (1992) was one of the first pieces she produced after graduating from the Rhode Island School of Design. It consisted of a 270-kg (600-lb) cube of chocolate and another of lard, both of which had been gnawed at, and a vitrine, titled 'Lipstick/Phenylethylamine Display', containing dozens of individual chocolates and red lipsticks, formed from the gnawed, chewed and then spat-out chocolate and lard. The enormous cubes, scarred with imprints of Antoni's teeth, mouth, nose and chin and juxtaposed with chocolates and lipstick – symbols of typically feminine desire – represented the 'female' as a primal mouth that gnaws and the 'feminine' as embodied by sweets and glossy red lips. *Gnaw* highlighted what the art critic and curator Laura Heon described as the 'disequilibrium between [Antoni's] violent devouring of these cubes and the expectations of what a "lady's" mouth should do'.[7]

For other artists, fat is used to explore the creative potential of waste. In Stelarc and Nina Sellars's *Blender* (2005), two containers rhythmically pumped bodily fluids, including the results of the liposuction procedures that both artists had undertaken specifically for the piece: 4.6 litres (4 qt) of fat taken from Stelarc's torso and Sellars's limbs. In a piece that has been described as one that illustrates the 'poetic materiality of bodily functions',[8] including digestion, *Blender* used 'excess' products to create a new technological 'body', one in which exchange between individual bodies – their blending and blurring in a biochemical soup – highlights the potential for the conventional boundaries and limits of the body to be dissolved, recreated and reimagined.

In Joseph Beuys's work, fat's abject materiality is reimagined as a point of access to the transformative and ritual potentials of physical matter. Beuys, who enjoyed cult status in Germany in the 1960s and '70s, first began to use fat in his sculptures in the early 1960s. In these works fat – a substance traditionally associated with excess and waste – served as an expression of the healing, warm, chaotic energy of the material world. In a fictionalized myth of origin that inspired many of the themes and materials used in his art, Beuys, a dive-bomber pilot for the Luftwaffe during the Second World War, claimed that his life was saved by nomadic Tartars when his plane crashed during a mission over the Crimean Peninsula in 1943. Finding him unconscious in the snow, the Tartars covered his body with fat and wrapped him in felt in order to regenerate his body warmth. While it was later revealed that Beuys was actually rescued by German soldiers and taken to a military hospital with neither fat nor felt, the story served as a structuring device for much of his art.

The theme of personal trauma appears in works such as *Bathtub* (1960), in which adhesive bandages and fat-soaked gauze are plastered onto the bathtub in which Beuys was bathed as a child. Like many of his works, the piece is not a representation of trauma but is instead a healing of it. Trauma is represented through healing substances: gauze, plasters and fat. For Beuys, fat is always a symbol of life and warmth because its malleability, its responsiveness to heat and its ability to move between solid and liquid states exemplifies the transformative power of materiality. Beuys's sculptural use of fat is perhaps best known through his *Fat Corner* series (1960–62) and his most well-known work, *Fat Chair* (1964). In *Fat Corner*, a large lump of fat – its transformability making it a material embodiment of chaos – is placed in a right-angled corner of a room, a constricting geometric form that mimics the extreme rationality of the modern world. *Fat Chair* – a chair with a block of fat placed on its seat – foregrounds our (often

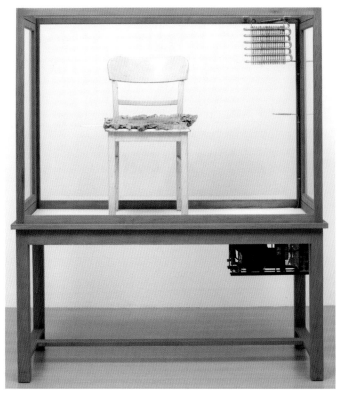

Joseph Beuys, *Fettstuhl* (Fat Chair), 1964.

displaced) relationship to materiality by connecting fat with
human digestive and excretive processes; the German title
of the work, *Fettstuhl*, plays on the connotations of *Stuhl*, or
stool, as a polite term for excrement.

While fats have had complex connotations in many forms
of popular cultural representation – simultaneously life-giving
and grotesque, both desirable and abject – they are sources of
unambiguous joy on food and lifestyle television programmes.
In recent years, fats have enjoyed growing prominence as

sources of pleasure, as celebrity television chefs promote the use of butter and lard several decades after health professionals in the West began to urge their reduction or elimination from the diet. The British 'Two Fat Ladies', Clarissa Dickson Wright and Jennifer Paterson, were among the first to pioneer the use of large amounts of butter, lard, dripping, bacon and cream on primetime television cooking shows and in best-selling cookbooks. Popular in the 1990s, the Ladies were openly subversive, revelling both in their own corpulence and in the carnivalesque excesses of the recipes they prepared. The back cover of *The Two Fat Ladies Ride Again* states that the 'Ladies laugh in the face of the fat-fearing fanatic', while *Two Fat Ladies: Obsessions* features a recipe for Chicken Jerusalem that includes a chicken, artichokes, 115 g (4 oz) of butter and 600 ml (1 pint) of double cream. The Ladies believed high-fat food to be one of life's great joys and comforts, with Dickson Wright once describing double cream as a greater mood enhancer than Prozac.[9] When Paterson died from cancer in 1999, halfway through filming the show's fourth series, an obituary in the *Daily Telegraph* described the Two Fat Ladies' abundant use of fat as 'an uncompromising sign of life being enjoyed'.

Pleasure is also foregrounded in Nigella Lawson's television shows and cookery books, in which she frequently plays with the connection between the sensual pleasures of food and sex. With sexy and flirtatious affectations, she groans with pleasure as she eats the food she cooks, and ends her episodes by joyously tucking in to the leftovers of the day's cooking (often at night and standing in front of the fridge) in a camp parody of 'secret' eating as women's 'guilty pleasure'. As it was for the Two Fat Ladies, this pleasure usually requires not scrimping on the fat, and using butter and cream as vehicles of comfort to escape the stresses and pressures of the modern world. In 2012 her programme *Nigellissima* shocked health professionals by featuring numerous fat-laden desserts, including a chocolate hazelnut cheesecake that contained a whopping 7,000 calories, or 583 calories per portion, and an ice cream brioche sandwich that contained 2,145 calories – more than the average recommended daily intake for a woman.[10] Despite (or perhaps because of) periodic criticisms, Lawson's combination of food, pleasure and excess has been highly lucrative, with the celebrity chef reported to have accrued £43.3 million in book sales alone.[11]

It is a formula that has also been successful for the American TV chef Emeril Lagasse, whose show *Emeril Live* had an eleven-year, every-weeknight run on the Food Network from 1997 to 2008. Lagasse combines working-class masculinity with a disdain for healthy eating edicts, preparing recipes made from a variety of fatty ingredients such as sausage, bacon, lard, cream and chocolate. He is known for popularizing the phrase 'Pork Fat Rules!', which was also the title of an *Emeril Live* episode featuring lard-laden recipes for andouille sausage, andouille-stuffed jalapeños, dirty black-eyed peas (so named for the dish's appearance following the addition of meat and spices) and pork *boulettes* (meatballs). Lagasse's exuberant personality emphasizes the pleasures of fat: for Lagasse, tasty food is at the centre of a life well-lived, not something we should deprive ourselves of to placate the 'nutrition police'.

Fats feature in an array of outrageous recipes by Paula Deen, the popular U.S. Food Network cooking show host and subject of numerous online parodies for her reputation as the 'Butter Queen'. Deep-fried lasagne, deep-fried cranberry sauce, deep-fried stuffing on a stick, deep-fried butter balls – the list goes on. When in 2012 she revealed on the American *Today* show that she had been diagnosed with type 2 diabetes three years earlier, she told host Al Roker that she is an entertainer and does not always eat the food she cooks on her show: 'Honey, I'm your cook, not your doctor', she told him.

The transgressive potential of fatty foods is perhaps taken to its ultimate conclusion in *Epic Meal Time*, an online cooking show that has been described as '*Jackass* in the kitchen'.[12] The series, which has over 6.5 million subscribers and has had over 700 million individual views of its videos, follows a group of men preparing enormous dishes of high-fat, high-calorie foods. Their recipe for a 'Fast Food Shepherd's Pie' comprises ten McDonald's double cheeseburgers, ten McChicken sandwiches, the patties from twenty double cheeseburgers and twenty Junior Chicken sandwiches, 1.3 kg (3 lb) of bacon, cheese and French fries. The show's Fat Counter tallied a massive 796 g (1½ lb) of fat and 11,150 calories for this dish. Similarly, the *Epic Meal Time* 'Fast Food Lasagna' is made from fifteen Big Macs, fifteen Wendy's Baconators, fifteen A&W's Teen Burgers, multiple trays of bacon, meat sauce and cheese, and clocks in at a massive 5,298 g (11½ lb) of fat and 62,948 calories. The show typically concludes with the men shovelling large portions of the finished dishes into their mouths, washed down with swigs of Jack Daniels.

Epic Meal Time's scenes of gorging are surprisingly remin-iscent of the feasting practices that were a feature of public life centuries earlier – only now, rather than a vehicle for the enactment of power, fats are now a source of entertainment. It is perhaps a fitting endpoint of the journey of fats: from an instrument of social hierarchy, to a lynchpin in debates about nutrition, health and the ethics of the food industry, to sources of comfort, critique and comedy in contemporary popular culture. Fats, foods both ordinary and essential for everyday life, offer rich symbolic repertoires that give them a fascinating place in both the cultural and the culinary imagination.

Recipes

Butter

500 ml (2 cups) double (heavy) cream
salt (optional)
iced water

Whip the cream until it splits into solids (butterfat) and liquid (buttermilk). Strain off the buttermilk and either discard or reserve for another use (such as making scones). Rinse the butter in iced water, then press to ensure all the water is removed. Add salt to taste.

Mayonnaise

2 egg yolks (use 60 g eggs)
2 tsp white wine vinegar
salt and pepper
250 ml (1 cup) neutral oil, such as rapeseed (canola)

Mix together the egg yolks and vinegar, and add salt and pepper to taste. Using either a hand (balloon) whisk or an electric beater, gradually whisk in the oil, a little at a time, until thick, pale and creamy.

Hot-water Pastry

575 g plain (all-purpose) flour
½ tsp salt
220 ml water
200 g lard

Sift the flour and salt into a bowl. Put the water and lard into a saucepan and bring to the boil; once boiling, pour it over the dry ingredients. Combine, and when the mixture is cool enough to handle (it should still be very warm) knead on a floured board until smooth. Form quickly into the shape required.

Makes enough for one large pie (serves 10)

Sweet Shortcrust Pastry

220 g (8 oz) plain flour
110 g (4 oz) unsalted butter
30 g (1 oz) sugar
1 medium egg
chilled water

Place the flour, butter and sugar into a bowl. Rub the butter into the flour until it resembles fine breadcrumbs. Add the egg and enough chilled water to bring the dough together. Knead quickly and gently until just smooth. Chill before forming into the shape required.

Makes enough to line a 28-cm tart tin

Joël Robuchon's *Purée de Pommes de Terre*

1 kg (2 lb) floury potatoes
100 ml (0.4 cups) milk, hot
200 g (7 oz) cold butter,
cut into cubes

Boil the potatoes. When cooked, mill them using a potato ricer and then push the milled potatoes through a drum sieve. Add the milk. Over a low heat, gradually add the butter. Once the butter is incorporated, whisk until the potatoes are light and fluffy.

Serves 6

Acarajé (Brazilian Black-eyed Bean Fritters)

400 g (2 cups) *feijão fradinho* (black-eyed beans)
1 onion, minced
30 g (¼ cup) ground dried shrimp (*camarão seco*)
salt and pepper
dendê (palm) oil, for frying

Soak the beans overnight, then remove and discard their outer skins. Using a food processor or mortar and pestle, mince or grind the beans. Add the onion, dried shrimp and salt and pepper to taste. Beat the mixture well. Once the oil is hot (around 180–190°C, 350–375°F), drop in spoonfuls of the batter. Cook until puffed and golden brown. Drain on paper towels. Traditionally served hot with *mojo de acareje*, a Brazilian-style chilli sauce.

Oliebollen (Dutch Doughnuts)

1 tsp dried active yeast
120 ml (½ cup) milk, warmed
150 g (1 cup) plain flour
1.5 tbsp sugar
1 tbsp butter, melted
1 egg
zest of ¼ lemon
salt
2 tbsp raisins, soaked overnight in rum
vegetable oil, for frying

Dissolve the yeast in the warm milk. Mix the flour, sugar, melted butter, egg, lemon zest and a pinch of salt in a bowl. Add the milk to it and mix, then stir in the rum-soaked raisins. Leave in a warm place to rise until doubled in size; stir, and then let rise again. Drop spoonfuls of the batter into the hot oil (approx 180–190°C, 350–375°F). Fry for 3–4 minutes on each side until golden brown. Drain on paper towels and sprinkle with icing sugar.

Mala Hotpot Broth
Adapted from Fuchsia Dunlop, *Sichuan Cookery*
(London, 2001)

50 g (2 oz) dried chillies
100 ml plus 3 tbsp groundnut (peanut) oil
200 g (7 oz) beef dripping (tallow)
100 g (3 ½ oz) Sichuan chilli bean paste
40 g (1 ½ oz) fermented black beans, mashed
40 g (1 ½ oz) fresh ginger, sliced
1.5 l (6 cups) beef stock
15 g (½ oz) rock sugar
90 ml (0.4 cups) Shaoxing rice wine
5 g Sichuan peppercorns
Salt

Sizzle the chillies in 3 tablespoons of the groundnut oil, drain and set aside. Gently heat the beef dripping and the remaining 100 ml groundnut oil in a wok until the dripping has melted. Increase the heat, then fry the chilli bean paste until the fat is a rich red colour. Add the mashed black beans and the ginger, and continue to stir fry until fragrant. Pour in the beef stock. Bring to the boil and add the sugar, Shaoxing wine, fried chillies, Sichuan peppercorns and salt to taste. Simmer for 15–20 minutes. Once the broth is ready, add dipping ingredients such as meat, offal, vegetables and bean curd to the hot sauce.

Serves 4–6

Fasolakia lathera (Braised Green Beans)

1 onion, chopped
60 ml (¼ cup) olive oil
220 g (8 oz) tomatoes, chopped
parsley, chopped
salt and pepper
450 g (1 lb) green beans
1 medium potato, chopped

Fry the onion in the olive oil. Add the chopped tomatoes, parsley, salt and pepper and bring to the boil. Add the beans and potato, then simmer until soft and tender (about 1 hour).

Serves 2–3

Dr Atkins's Peaches and Cream Omelette
Adapted from Robert C. Atkins, *The Illustrated Atkins New Diet Cookbook* (London, 2004), p. 41

220 g (8 oz) full-fat cream cheese
8 large eggs
60 ml (¼ cup) double (heavy) cream
2 tbsp sugar substitute
salt
30 g (1 oz) butter
5 tbsp chopped tinned or poached peaches

Combine the cream cheese, eggs, double cream, sugar substitute and a pinch of salt in a bowl. Heat the butter in a large frying pan and cook the omelette mixture in it. When the centre is firm, spoon peaches over the centre and fold over the sides. Slide out of the pan and serve.

Serves 4

Pörkölt (Hungarian Stew)

1 onion, chopped
2 tbsp lard
1 heaped tbsp sweet paprika powder
1 tsp salt
1 kg (2 lb) red meat, diced
1 large tomato, peeled and diced
1 green bell pepper, diced

Fry the onion in the lard. Mix in the paprika and salt, and add the meat. Let the meat cook gently in its own steam, adding a few tablespoons of water as needed. Once the meat starts to soften, add the tomato and green pepper. Cook until the meat is tender. Allow the gravy to reduce as much as possible without burning the stew. *Traditionally served with buttered noodles. Serves 5–6*

Paula Deen's Fried Butter Balls
Adapted from www.pauladeen.com, accessed 14 August 2014

100 g (2 sticks) unsalted butter
55 g (2 oz) cream cheese
salt and pepper
120 g (1 cup) plain (all-purpose) flour
1 egg, beaten
120 g (1 cup) seasoned breadcrumbs
oil, for frying

Whisk the butter, cream cheese, and salt and pepper to taste with an electric mixer until smooth. Using a small ice-cream scoop or melon-baller, form the butter mixture into 1-inch balls. Arrange balls on a baking tray and freeze until solid. Coat the frozen balls in flour, dip in beaten egg and then coat in breadcrumbs. Freeze again. Fry the balls for 10–15 seconds in hot oil (approx 180°C, 375°F) until light-golden. Drain on paper towels. Serve as a snack or appetizer.

References

1 Power and Prestige: Fats in History

1 Loren Cordain et al., 'Plant–Animal Subsistence Ratios and Macronutrient Energy Estimations in Worldwide Hunter-gatherer Diets', *American Journal of Clinical Nutrition*, LXXI (2000), pp. 682–92.

2 Miki Ben-Dor et al., 'Man the Fat Hunter: The Demise of *Homo erectus* and the Emergence of a New Hominin Lineage in the Middle Pleistocene (ca. 400 kyr) Levant', *PLOS One*, VI/12 (2011), pp. 1–12.

3 Vilhjalmur Stefansson, *The Fat of the Land* [1956] (New York, 1960), p. 31.

4 John D. Speth, 'Seasonality, Resource Stress, and Food Sharing in So-called "Egalitarian" Foraging Societies', *Journal of Anthropological Archaeology*, IX (1990), pp. 148–88.

5 Felipe Fernández-Armesto, *Food: A History* (London, 2002), p. 120.

6 Roy Strong, *Feast: A History of Grand Eating* (London, 2003), p. 88.

7 Paul Lacroix, *Manners, Customs, and Dress during the Middle Ages, and during the Renaissance Period* (New York, 1874), p. 73.

8 Kathy L. Pearson, 'Nutrition and the Early-Medieval Diet', *Speculum*, LXXII (1997), pp. 1–32.

9 Stewart Lee Allen, *In the Devil's Garden: A Sinful History of*

Forbidden Food (Edinburgh, 2002), pp. 249–50.
10 Christopher E. Forth, 'The Qualities of Fat: Bodies, History, and Materiality', *Journal of Material Culture*, xviii/2 (2013), pp. 135–54.

2 Fats around the World: Cooking with Fat

1 Fuchsia Dunlop, *Sichuan Cookery* (London, 2003), p. xliv.
2 Rachel E. Gross, 'Keepers of the Oil: The Science of Fried', www.the-sieve.com, 3 October 2013.
3 Carey Polis, 'John Alleman Dead: Heart Attack Grill Unofficial Spokesman Dies from Heart Attack', *Huffington Post*, 13 February 2013.

3 Nutritional Science Weighs In: The Changing Fate of Fats

1 Ancel Keys et al., 'The Diet and 15-year Death Rate in the Seven Countries Study', *American Journal of Epidemiology*, cxxiv (1986), pp. 903–15.
2 'Medicine: The Fat of the Land', *Time* (13 January 1961), pp. 30–34.
3 Norman Jolliffe, 'Fats, Cholesterol, and Coronary Heart Disease: A Review of Recent Progress', *Circulation*, xx (1959), pp. 109–27.
4 Mary Enig, 'The Tragic Legacy of Center for Science in the Public Interest', www.westonaprice.org, 6 January 2003.
5 Ronald P. Mensink and Martijn B. Katan, 'Effect of Dietary Trans Fatty Acids on High-density and Low-density Lipoprotein Cholesterol Levels in Healthy Subjects', *New England Journal of Medicine*, cccxxiii (1990), pp. 439–45.
6 Walter C. Willett et al., 'Intake of Trans Fatty Acids and Risk of Coronary Heart Disease among Women', *The Lancet*, cccxlv/8845 (1993), pp. 581–5.
7 Walter C. Willett and Albert Ascherio, 'Trans Fatty Acids:

Are the Effects only Marginal?', *American Journal of Public Health*, LXXXIV (1994), pp. 722–4.

8 Roberto A. Ferdman, 'Margarine of Error: The War against Butter is Over. Butter Won', www.qz.com, 20 January 2014.

9 David Schleifer, 'The Perfect Solution: How Trans Fats became the Healthy Replacement for Saturated Fats', *Technology and Culture*, LIII (2012), pp. 94–119.

10 World Cancer Research Fund, 'Scientists "Always Changing their Minds" on Cancer', www.wcrf-org, 25 May 2009.

11 David Pierson, 'Butter Consumption in U.S. Hits 40-year High', www.latimes.com, 7 January 2014.

12 National Institutes of Health, *Morbidity and Mortality: 2012 Chart Book on Cardiovascular, Lung, and Blood Diseases* (Bethesda, MD, 2012).

13 Ankur Pandya et al., 'More Americans Living Longer with Cardiovascular Disease will Increase Costs while Lowering Quality of Life', *Health Affairs*, XXXII (2013), pp. 1706–14.

14 A. M. Salter, 'Dietary Fatty Acids and Cardiovascular Disease', *Animal*, VII (2013), pp. 163–71.

15 Kim Severson and Melanie Warner, 'Fat Substitute is Pushed Out of the Kitchen', www.nytimes.com, 13 February 2005.

16 Zoe Harcombe, Julien S. Baker and Bruce Davies, 'Food for Thought: Have We Been Giving the Wrong Dietary Advice?', *Food and Nutrition Science*, IV (2013), pp. 240–44.

17 World Health Organization, 'Controlling the Global Obesity Epidemic', www.who.int, accessed 6 August 2014.

18 A. W. Pennington, 'Treatment of Obesity with Calorically Unrestricted Diets', *Journal of Clinical Nutrition*, 1/5 (1953), pp. 343–8.

19 Robert C. Atkins, *Dr Atkins' New Diet Revolution* (London, 1992), pp. 29, 138–9.

20 Ibid., p. 25.

21 USDA National Nutrient Database for Standard Reference, http://ndb.nal.usda.gov, accessed 6 August 2014.

22 Harcombe, Baker and Davies, 'Food for Thought'.

23 Lee Hooper et al., 'Dietary Fat Intake and Prevention of

Cardiovascular Disease: Systematic Review', *BMJ*, CCCXXII (2001), pp. 757–63.

24 Lee Hooper et al., 'Reduced or Modified Dietary Fat for Preventing Cardiovascular Disease', *Cochrane Database of Systematic Reviews*, V (2012), CD002137.

25 Patty W. Siri-Tarino et al., 'Meta-analysis of Prospective Cohort Studies Evaluating the Association of Saturated Fat with Cardiovascular Disease', *American Journal of Clinical Nutrition*, XCI (2010), pp. 535–46.

26 Rajiv Chowdhury et al., 'Association of Dietary, Circulating, and Supplement Fatty Acids with Coronary Risk', *Annals of Internal Medicine*, CLX (2014), pp. 398–406.

27 'New Evidence Raises Questions about the Link between Fatty Acids and Heart Disease', www.cam.ac.uk, accessed 6 August 2014.

28 Siri-Tarino et al., 'Meta-analysis of Prospective Cohort Studies'.

4 Manufacturing Fats:
Low-fat, No-fat, Artificial Fat

1 Felipe Fernández-Armesto, *Food: A History* (London, 2002), p. 227.

2 Geoffrey P. Miller, 'Public Choice at the Dawn of the Special Interest State: The Story of Butter and Margarine', *California Law Review*, LXXVII (1989), pp. 83–131.

3 Gerry Strey, 'The "Oleo Wars": Wisconsin's Fight over the Demon Spread', *Wisconsin Magazine of History*, LXXXV/1 (Autumn 2001), pp. 3–15.

4 G. R. List and M. A. Jackson, 'The Battle over Hydrogenation (1903–1920)', *Inform*, XVIII/6 (2007), pp. 403–5.

5 Herbert J. Dutton and John C. Cowan, 'The Flavor Problem of Soybean Oil', in *The Yearbook of Agriculture, 1950–1951: Crops in Peace and War*, ed. Alfred Stefferud (Washington, DC, 1951), pp. 575–8.

6 Fereidoon Shahidi, ed., *Bailey's Industrial Oil and Fat Products*,

6th edn (Hoboken, NJ, 2005), p. 4.

7 Emily Waltz, 'Food Firms Test Fry Pioneer's Trans Fat-free Soybean Oil', *Nature Biotechnology*, XXVIII/8 (2010), pp. 769–70.

8 American Soybean Association, 'Tentative Determination Regarding Partially Hydrogenated Oils', www.soygrowers.com, accessed 1 September 2014.

9 Ibid.

10 Marion Nestle, *Food Politics: How the Food Industry Influences Nutrition and Health* (Berkeley, CA, 2002), p. 330.

11 Helena Gylling et al., 'Plant Sterols and Plant Stanols in the Management of Dyslipidaemia and Prevention of Cardiovascular Disease', *Atherosclerosis*, CCXXXII (2014), pp. 346–60.

12 Sedef Nehir El and Sebnem Simsek, 'Food Technological Applications for Optimal Nutrition: An Overview of Opportunities for the Food Industry', *Comprehensive Reviews in Food Science and Safety*, XI (2012), pp. 2–12.

13 Nestle, *Food Politics*, p. 300.

14 Judy Putnam, Jane Allshouse and Linda Scott Kantor, 'U.S. Per Capita Food Supply Trends: More Calories, Refined Carbohydrates, and Fats', *FoodReview*, XXV/3 (2002), pp. 2–15.

15 Jane Allshouse, Betsy Frazao and John Turpening, 'Are Americans Turning Away from Lower Fat Salty Snacks?' *FoodReview*, XXV/3 (2002), pp. 38–42.

16 S. Tuomasjukka, M. Viitanen and H. Kallio, 'Stearic Acid is Well Absorbed from Short- and Long-acyl-chain Triacylglycerol in an Acute Test Meal', *European Journal of Clinical Nutrition*, LXI (2007), pp. 1352–8.

17 David E. Newton, *Food Chemistry* (New York, 2007), p. 82.

18 John Byczkowski and Cliff Peale, 'FDA Lifts Olestra Warnings: Snacks No Longer Need Labels about Side Effects', *Cincinnati Enquirer*, www.enquirer.com, 2 August 2003.

19 Ibid.

20 Michael Pollan, *In Defence of Food* (London 2008), p. 1.

21 Ibid., p. 143.

22 David Pierson, 'Butter Consumption in U.S. Hits 40-year High', www.latimes.com, 7 January 2014.

23 Shahidi, ed., *Bailey's Industrial Oil and Fat Products*, p. 178.

24 Sherri Brooks Vinton and Ann Clark Espuelas, *The Real Food Revival* (New York, 2005), p. 122.

25 See Mount Gnomon Farm, at www.mountgnomonfarm.blogspot.com.au, accessed 6 August 2014.

5 Desire and Defilement: Fats in Popular Culture

1 Kenneth Grahame, *The Wind in the Willows* (London, 1959), p. 163.

2 Wendy R. Katz, 'Some Uses of Food in Children's Literature', *Children's Literature in Education*, XI/4 (1980), pp. 192–9.

3 Enid Blyton, *Upper Fourth at Malory Towers* (London, 1949), p. 64.

4 Enid Blyton, *Five Run Away Together* (London, 1944), p. 22.

5 Susan Honeyman, 'Gastronomic Utopias: The Legacy of Political Hunger in African American Lore', *Children's Literature*, XXXVIII (2010), pp. 44–63.

6 Toni Morrison, *Beloved* (London, 1987), p. 70.

7 Laura Heon, 'Janine Antoni's Gnawing Idea', *Gastronomica: The Journal of Food and Culture*, 1/2 (2001), pp. 5–8.

8 Daniel Tércio, 'Martyrium as Performance', *Performance Research*, XV/1 (2010), pp. 90–99.

9 Sherrie A. Inness, *Secret Ingredients: Race, Gender, and Class at the Dinner Table* (New York, 2006), p. 178.

10 Alasdair Glennie, 'Nigella's Desserts Pack a Paunch', *The Advertiser* (4 October 2012), p. 57.

11 Chris Hall, 'Jamie Oliver to Nigella Lawson: Who's Been Cooking the Books?', www.dailymail.co.uk, 3 March 2012.

12 Mike Boone, 'Men Gone Wild – with Food', www.montrealgazette.com, 19 January 2011.

Select Bibliography

Barer-Stein, Thelma, *You Eat what You Are: People, Culture and Food Traditions* (Toronto, 1999)

Fernández-Armesto, Felipe, *Food: A History* (London, 2002)

Grigson, Jane, ed., *World Atlas of Food: A Gourmet's Guide to the Great Regional Dishes of the World* (London, 1974)

McLagan, Jennifer, *Fat: An Appreciation of a Misunderstood Ingredient, with Recipes* (New York, 2008)

Nestle, Marion, *Food Politics: How the Food Industry Influences Nutrition and Health* (Berkeley, CA, 2002)

Newton, David E., *Food Chemistry* (New York, 2007)

Schleifer, David, 'The Perfect Solution: How Trans Fats became the Healthy Replacement for Saturated Fats', *Technology and Culture*, LIII (2012), pp. 94–119

Tannahill, Reay, *Food in History* (New York, 1988)

Taubes, Gary, *Good Calories, Bad Calories: Fats, Carbs and the Controversial Science of Diet and Health* (New York, 2008)

Toussaint-Samat, Maguelonne, *A History of Food*, trans. Andrea Bell (Malden, MA, 1994)

Websites and Associations

American Heart Association
www.heart.org

BanTransFats.com
www.bantransfats.com

British Lard Marketing Board (spoof website)
www.britishlard.co.uk

Center for Science in the Public Interest
www.cspinet.org

Cyberlipid Center
www.cyberlipid.org

European Livestock Breeds Ark and Rescue Net (ELBARN)
www.elbarn.net

Fatworks (U.S.-based mail order fats company)
www.fatworksfoods.com

Heart Foundation of Australia
www.heartfoundation.org.au

USDA National Nutrient Database
http://ndb.nal.usda.gov

Acknowledgements

Research for this book was supported by the Australian Research Council (DE140101412) and the University of Tasmania's Environment Research Group. I would like to thank Andrew F. Smith and Michael Leaman for the opportunity to contribute to the Edible series; George Phillipov for sending me countless references to 'fat' and for helping me get to grips with the medical literature that forms the basis of Chapter Three; Erin Hawley, John Cianchi and Peter Wells for their assistance securing the images and image permissions for the book; Hannah Stark for her helpful feedback on the draft manuscript; and Simon Koop for travelling with me on this journey into the weird and wonderful world of fat.

Photo Acknowledgements

The author and publishers wish to express their thanks to the below sources of illustrative material and / or permission to reproduce it.

Image courtesy of The Advertising Archives: p. 76; © Janine Antoni; courtesy of the artist and Luhring Augustine, New York: p. 100; Ari N/Shutterstock: p. 80; the author: pp. 58, 59, 81; Bibliotheque des Arts Decoratifs, Paris, France/Archives Charmet /Bridgeman Images: p. 18; Bigstock.com: p. 16 (Banet), p. 57 (flippo), p. 87 (Samphire), p. 96 (Delmas Lehman), frontispiece (digitalista); © Bidouze Stéphane/Dreamstime: p. 47; © Paul Brighton/Dreamstime: p. 43; © Mary Ebersold/Dreamstime: p. 46; Eide Collection, Anchorage Museum, B1970.028.17: p. 10; © Ermess/Dreamstime: p. 32; ffolas/Shutterstock: p. 41; Fran/ www.CartoonStock.com: p. 61; © Getty Images/ FOX Image Collection: p. 99; © Gillrivers/Dreamstime: p. 38; Ralph Hagen/ www.CartoonStock.com: p. 56; iStock.com/ookpiks: p. 28; Kamira/ Shutterstock: p. 14; khanbm52/Shutterstock: p. 85; Tina Larsson/ Shutterstock: p. 64; © David Lloyd/Dreamstime: p. 31; © Carlo Mari/Age Fotostock: p. 11; Mary Evans Picture Library: p. 72; Jorgen McLeman/Shutterstock: p. 93; Michal Modzelewski/ Shutter-stock: p. 39; Juanan Barros Moreno/Shutterstock: p. 86; National Galleries of Scotland and Tate. Acquired jointly through The d'Offay Donation with assistance from the National Heritage Memorial Fund and the Art Fund 2008. © Joseph Beuys/Bild-Kunst. Licensed

Index

italic numbers refer to illustrations; **bold** to recipes